A Covenant Kiss

Dana Hemminger

A Covenant Kiss

Copyright © 2016 by Dana Hemminger

All rights reserved.

Back cover author photograph by Shelly Tate-Photography

For additional copies, visit www.amazon.com

Scripture taken from the New King James Version ®. Copyright © 1982 by Thomas Nelson. Used by permission. All rights reserved.

Printed in the United States of America

ISBN-13: 978-1523466863

ISBN-10: 1523466863

Dedication

I dedicate this book to my three amazing children: Benjamin, Joelle, and Josiah. You are each a priceless treasure to your dad and me. Your lives are a beautiful testimony of our love and union as husband and wife, and we are so honored that we were chosen to be your parents! May you live lives of integrity and purity, confident in who God has created you to be!

"Keep your heart with all diligence, for out of it spring the issues of life." –Proverbs 4:23

Table of Contents

Introduction — 1
Prologue — 4

1. Broken Homes, Broken Hearts — 7
2. A Father in Heaven — 11
3. Searching for Identity — 15
4. Trying to Fill the Void — 18
5. The Power of Prayer — 23
6. College Days — 28
7. Life-Changing Experiences — 33
8. Clutching the Old Security Blanket — 40
9. Poetry of Pain and Praise — 48
10. Emotions Can Be Deceiving — 59
11. Paths Prepared to Meet — 68
12. You Could Marry Him Someday! — 75
13. Chocolate Chip Cookies — 77
14. A Season for Love? — 81
15. Testing the Boundaries — 90
16. Purity: The Heart of the Matter — 95
17. Surrender — 98
18. You're Going to Chase Me Now! — 104
19. I Am My Beloved's and He is Mine — 109
20. Dream Come True — 116
21. Forgiveness and Repentance: The Two-Sided Coin — 122
22. Healing Prayers — 135
23. A Night for Grace — 140

End Notes	151
About the Author	153

Introduction

If you are holding this book in your hands right now, you have a reason for doing so. Perhaps you know Shawn and me and are interested in learning more about our story. Perhaps the title caught your attention and stirred your curiosity. Perhaps you are young and single, dreaming of a future "happily ever after." Perhaps you are living with pain and regret, your heart shipwrecked on the often deadly rocks of romantic love. To you especially, I would say there is grace and forgiveness, healing and second chances. Whatever your reason for reading, I'm glad you've chosen to do so!

Sadly, we live in a culture that idolizes sex, promoting and applauding promiscuity while scoffing at sexual purity. Living without restraint in the area of romantic love is viewed as a normal and healthy "freedom of expression." In contrast, living with self-control and morality is often viewed with disdain as "radical" and "extreme." As a Christian teenager in the 1990's, the propaganda of this culture of sex was all around me. These pressures have only intensified since the turn of the century as pop culture and political correctness race head first into the ideals of moral relativism and the sentiment, "If it feels good, do it!" Marriage itself has recently come under great attack in our nation, as an increasingly progressive culture seeks to re-define a sacred covenant created by God Himself. Those who desire to go against this tide will often face opposition and criticism at every turn. This generation is faced with the questions, "Is living a life of sexual purity relevant or even worth it? If so, what is such a lifestyle to even look like?"

There have been many excellent books written on the subject of sexual purity and dating. I am not seeking to re-write one of these books. My desire in writing this book is to share a real-life story of heartbreak, healing, and a love worth fighting for. I am opening the door of vulnerability and honesty as I share my personal journey in the area of romantic love, with the mistakes and triumphs along the way and the power of grace to overcome in all things. Whatever season of life you may be walking through, my hope is that our story will inspire you to believe that not only is purity possible today, it is relevant, it is beautiful, and it is ultimately fulfilling. Thanks for reading…

Love suffers long and is kind; love does not envy; love does not parade itself, is not puffed up; does not behave rudely, does not seek its own, is not provoked, thinks no evil; does not rejoice in iniquity, but rejoices in the truth; bears all things, believes all things, hopes all things, endures all things. Love never fails... (1 Corinthians 13:4-8a).

Prologue

Gentle Christmas music played quietly in the church sanctuary as guests began to arrive, creating an atmosphere of warmth and peace. Festive wreaths, sweeping ribbons and small evergreens wrapped in soft, white lights added graceful beauty to this December wedding day. As the music continued, the wedding party began their march down the aisle. Two proud mothers each lit a candle, one representing a daughter and the other a son. An eager and nervous groom waited expectantly at the altar for the unveiling of his bride. A song by Twila Paris entitled *How Beautiful* began to play as the bridesmaids, dressed in shining gowns of deep red satin, made their entrance. As the song reached verse three, the double doors opened again, the guests stood, and the radiant bride emerged in her beautiful white gown that shimmered with delicate rhinestones, her face aglow with joy.

How beautiful the radiant bride

Who waits for her groom with His light in her eyes*

A beaming groom made his way down the aisle and took the hand of his cherished bride, gently leading her back up the aisle to the altar as a symbolic gesture of the magnificent day when Jesus Christ will return for His beloved Bride and lead her to glory.

How beautiful when humble hearts give

The fruit of pure lives so that others may live

How beautiful, how beautiful

How beautiful is the Body of Christ.*

The wedding ceremony was a touching one full of testimony and loving exhortation, communion, and the exchange of vows both traditional and personally written by the bride and groom. There were laughter and tears throughout the sanctuary as friends and family happily took part in the celebration. From the moment his bride made her entrance, the groom could not stop gazing at her. He scarcely heard the words that were being shared, so intent was he on his beloved.

Finally, the moment everyone had been waiting for arrived. The air was thick with anticipation as the minister shared the couple's unique choice. During their two years of courtship, they had decided to save their very first kiss for their wedding day. Grinning from ear to ear, the minister spoke the longed-for words, "You may now kiss your bride!" No sooner was the phrase out of his mouth than the groom drew his bride close. Time seemed to stand still as their lips met for the first time, and the church erupted in applause and cheers. Unable to contain his delight, the groom did a little hop, to which the minister responded, "I think you'd better kiss her again!" He needed no more convincing and drew her close once more. As their lips met again, two years of longing reached fulfillment, and two lives were knit together in covenant relationship with a lifetime of discovery yet to unfold. This is their story…

*Paris, Twila. "How Beautiful." Lyrics. <u>8 Greatest Hits.</u> Sparrow, 2004.

1
Broken Homes, Broken Hearts

The girl was young, petite and beautiful, but much of life was a struggle. The atmosphere at home was usually tense. Her mother was often ill and very depressed. Her father was passive and emotionally distant. Searching for meaning, she immersed herself in the social life high school could offer. There she met a young man who was strong, yet gentle and so attentive. He made her feel secure, important and powerful. She didn't necessarily love him, but she loved how he made her feel. However, when she discovered she was pregnant with a son, getting married seemed like the right thing to do. The two teens were wed and entered a rocky marriage.

Within a few years a second little boy arrived. The young mother tried to hold on for a few more years, but she was so unhappy in the relationship.

While her small sons were still pre-school age, she filed for a divorce. The young father was crushed and slipped further into his introverted state. The little boys didn't understand what was happening, but their growing up years became ones of joint custody—one week with Mom, one week with Dad. Mom worked hard and returned to school to obtain a nursing degree in order to better provide for her children. As a result, though, her boys didn't get to see her much during their younger years. Dad also worked hard to provide, but he was emotionally distant and shut-down. Both parents loved their sons fiercely and were doing the best they knew in the midst of their own pain and brokenness. Both boys grew up struggling with anger and longing for affirmation, affection and a sense of identity.

******

The young woman was in her twenties. Life had been a hard one with an abusive and then absent father and a hard-working but emotionally distant mother. She wrestled with low self-esteem and longed to find a place of purpose and belonging. As a high school student she had been drawn into a religious cult that seemed to offer her both.

The young man was also in his twenties. He grew up in the same religious cult, but his home was not a happy one. Though married, his parents' marriage was very dysfunctional, and he experienced physical and emotional abuse from multiple family members. He threw himself intensely into his religion, searching for the same sense of purpose and belonging.

The young man and young woman met at a religious conference. They were drawn to each other by their own sense of neediness and wanting to be needed. A long distance relationship began, leading to engagement and ultimately marriage, though they had spent very little time together. The marriage started out fairly well, but the brokenness each one carried into the marriage was only perpetuated in their new life together. Within a few years a daughter was born, and they were thrilled. However, the next two years were marked by deep pain and betrayal. The young mother felt obligated to hang on for the sake of their daughter, and shortly after a son was born, only adding to her sense of duty. Poverty seemed to be their constant companion, and soon she gained the courage to pursue graduate school. Upon obtaining her degree, she was offered a teaching job in another state, and the family left the only home they had known.

Once settled into their new life, the mother kept trying to hold on for the sake of her children, but within a couple years she realized she couldn't hang on any longer and filed for a divorce. Her children were age eight and five. The father, who already struggled with depression, was completely devastated. He soon moved across the state. Though he loved his children very much, his own pain and financial struggle kept him away, and he only saw them a few times a year. The daughter and son were shocked and confused, hurting and angry. They missed their father desperately. To their young hearts, his distance felt like rejection.

2
A Father In Heaven

The first year after my parents' divorce is mostly a blur in my memory. The heartache I experienced led to depression. My emotional pain affected my physical health, and I missed so much school during my third and fourth grade years, it's amazing that I passed. There were days I would literally *will* myself to feel sick just so I wouldn't have to go to school. Meanwhile my mom was trying to get her bearings as a single parent. She had residential custody of my brother and me, though she was very eager to give us opportunity to visit our dad when he was able. Her heart was breaking to see the pain we were experiencing in his absence. She never imagined that he would withdraw from our lives to such a degree.

Desperate for support and searching for answers, she decided to leave the religious cult we had been a part of for so long and began taking us to visit evangelical churches on Sundays. She was insecure, wondering how we would be received with her recent divorce and religious background. However, one church in particular welcomed us with open and loving arms, receiving us as their own. We began attending regularly. My mom would weep through every service as truth and love poured into her weary soul.

My brother and I were involved in the children's ministry program where we were introduced to the Gospel. The religious cult we had been a part of talked about Jesus but not as Savior. Individual performance and perfection were the main focus and the means of justification. Now I was learning that Jesus died on the cross for my sins, and I could be forgiven for them all. I didn't have to try to be perfect on my own, a huge relief after living under the weight of such an impossible goal. Instead, I was made right with God by believing in Jesus and accepting His free gift of salvation! I was also learning that God is a Father who loves me, which brought comfort to my young heart in the midst of my sorrow over my Dad's absence. However, I was also angry with my parents for teaching me lies all my life. It was hard for me to understand that they were teaching my brother and me the only "truth" they knew at the time.

Within the first year of attending our new church, my mom, my brother and I had all asked Jesus to forgive us of our sins and to come into our hearts as our Lord and Savior. My dad also experienced the same where he was living. Though there was still much healing that needed to take place in our lives, this was a pivotal turning point for us all. God was already starting to bring good out of our painful situation.

******

Meanwhile, in another part of the country, Shawn was a little boy full of insecurity and anger. To cope he developed quite a "potty mouth," and he often bullied other children, that is, until they got bigger than him! Though his mother's childhood was dysfunctional, she had grown up attending church but then walked away during her teenage years. One spring as she drove across town with her two sons, now in elementary school, she asked them, "Do you guys know what Easter is about?" They promptly replied, "The Easter Bunny and candy!" She was suddenly convicted that her boys were growing up knowing nothing about God. She decided that they should all begin attending church together. Shawn and his brother were resistant, complaining that they couldn't sleep in on Sundays anymore and resentful that they had to sit through services that bored them, but she persisted.

One morning, alone in her kitchen, this young mother knelt down on the floor and recommitted her life to Christ. A peaceful contentment flooded her soul, and she no longer felt alone. In time she would marry another man and have a third son. She continued to take her boys to church week after week, though it would be years before Shawn would truly discover the God who loves him.

3
Searching for Identity

Every little girl grows up with a deep desire planted inside of her to be beautiful. She wants to be considered a treasure worthy of pursuit. She longs to feel protected, affirmed, and cherished. These are God-given desires, woven into her very DNA. Her heart is drawn to the fairytales of the beautiful princess pursued by the valiant prince, because in her heart of hearts she knows she was made to be a princess. Likewise, little boys grow up longing to be the hero and to know that they "have what it takes" to be a man. They are drawn to the stories of the warriors--those strong and brave, living with purpose. They long for significance. In His grand design, these desires are meant to be nourished in youth by intentional and loving parents, in adulthood by a loving spouse, and ultimately by God Himself.

However, we live in the midst of a broken world, full of broken hearts and broken homes. Fathers especially are meant to speak identity into the lives of their children. However, many are unable fulfill this role because true fatherhood was never modeled for them. They bring their own wounds and faulty mindsets into their families (as do mothers). They cannot give what they themselves have not received, and the unhealthy cycles are often perpetuated generation to generation. As a result, children are left wondering who they really are and searching to fill the voids inside, often in very unhealthy ways. God longs to heal these hurts and fill these empty places in the hearts of people, but many are not aware of their need for healing or how to receive it. This was my story…

I was a Christian, and I knew in my head that God loved me, but my heart was still full of hurt, rejection and a growing bitterness toward my dad for his absence in my life. To increase matters, I was shy and sometimes awkward as a child, which made me a target of ridicule among my peers. As a result, my self-esteem was very low, so I threw myself into performance, a tendency already deeply engrained in me from early childhood. I was able to excel in academics, and since I wasn't receiving the affirmation I longed for from my dad and my peers, I sought it from my teachers and other authority figures in my life. I enjoyed music and joined the school band as a percussionist during my fifth grade year, continuing to play through the rest of my years in school. I never felt pressure from my mom to perform, and I felt secure in her love, but an internal drive to perform for acceptance had a deep root inside of me.

My performance orientation over-shadowed my Christian walk as well, as I sought to always do the right thing and be the "good little Christian girl." My identity was completely wrapped up in how well I could perform in any given area, and I was constantly in fear of being a disappointment to those around me, including God. I knew in my head that His love was unconditional, but the reality in my heart was that He could only be pleased with me if I was getting everything right. When I felt like I was doing well, I hid in pride to try and compensate for my deep insecurities. When I felt like I had messed up in any way I was plagued by feelings of guilt and shame that only increased as I got older. I was walking a destructive path of which I was unaware.

4
Trying to Fill the Void

With a longing in my heart to feel significant, valued, and protected, I turned to boys early on. From age twelve to age eighteen I dated three different boys. During those six years I was only single for around eight to nine months, and that wasn't all at once! I clung to these immature relationships, aching to fill the hole in my heart. I had the right words and theology; I could *say* that Jesus was the One who met my needs and that He was my best friend. Since I could say this, I deceived myself into believing I was living this truth, when in reality, I was looking to my boyfriend to meet the deepest needs inside of me. I was living in idolatry and didn't even know it. Since I was a Christian, I only dated boys who professed to be Christians as well. Two of them were even sons of pastors, and one was a brand new Christian, but each of them struggled with their own places of insecurity, pain and brokenness. I wanted to spend as much time with them as possible, allowing my life to revolve around the relationship and neglecting other friendships in the process. As Christians, we agreed that sex was to be reserved for marriage, but poor boundaries, time spent alone, and teenage hormones resulted in some very poor choices. By the grace of God, we all maintained our virginity, but we were not living sexually pure lifestyles.

When I was seventeen I was volunteering regularly at a small Christian book and music store called "Tunes for Christ." The owner gave all his volunteer staff an in-store discount as well as the freedom to read any of the books in the store as long as we kept them in good condition. One afternoon business was especially slow, and I had a few hours alone before my boyfriend came to pick me up. There was a particular book I had been trying hard to ignore. *I Kissed Dating Goodbye*, written by Joshua Harris, had recently hit the market, and it was creating a lot of buzz. Just the title made me cringe inside, but I felt drawn to it as well. I was at the height of entanglement and compromise with my current boyfriend. I felt the conviction of the Holy Spirit, but I didn't have the resolve to make the drastic changes that were needed. On this particular day, I finally picked up the book and started to read. Everything inside of me was screaming, but I couldn't put it down either. The Lord was using the author's words to hit deep places in my heart. He had me from the introduction:

> Thanks for picking up this book. Some people never get past the title...I don't want to argue with you about whether or not you should date. Yes, I'll be honest about the problems I see in the way most people date today. But ultimately my goal isn't to convince you to stop dating. I want to help you examine the aspects of your life that dating touches—the way you treat others, the way you prepare for your future mate, your personal purity—and look at what it means to bring these areas in line with God's Word.[1]

Joshua Harris goes on to talk about the "Little Relationship Principle: The joy of intimacy is the reward of commitment."[2] He makes the strong point that people in dating relationships are often selfishly seeking to have personal needs met and to enjoy the feelings of intimacy, whether emotional or physical, without the commitment necessary for true intimacy. Harris says, "I've come to realize that while friendships with the opposite sex are great, I have no business asking for a girl's heart and exclusive affections if I'm not ready to consider marriage."[3]

When I came to the chapter titled "The Seven Habits of Highly Defective Dating," I realized I could check off almost every one:

1. Dating tends to skip the friendship stage of a relationship...
2. Dating often mistakes a physical relationship for love...
3. Dating often isolates a couple from other vital relationships...
4. Dating can distract young adults from their primary responsibility of preparing for the future...
5. Dating can cause discontentment with God's gift of singleness...
6. Dating can create an artificial environment for evaluating another person's character...
7. Dating often becomes an end in itself...[4]

I was equally challenged by his "Five Attitude Changes to Avoid Defective Dating":

1. Every relationship is an opportunity to model Christ's love...
2. My unmarried years are a gift from God...
3. I don't need to pursue a romantic relationship before I'm ready for marriage...
4. I cannot "own" someone outside of marriage...

5. I will avoid situations that could compromise the purity of my body or mind…[5]

Now my goal is not to re-write Joshua Harris' book. I quote the things I do in order to share how the Lord was using this book to speak to my heart as a teenage girl. He was gently pointing out to me the unhealthy pattern I had become a slave to, and He was inviting me to greater freedom. By the time my boyfriend came to pick me up that day, I was under so much conviction that I had to tell him right then and there what I was reading my growing concerns. He didn't understand much of what I was telling him, but ultimately our relationship came to an end. Since we had unwisely given each other so much of our affection emotionally and physically, this was very painful for us both, but I knew the pain would be greater if we continued in the destructive direction we were heading. I was beginning a journey to freedom, but there would still be many bumps in the road and hard lessons to learn.

5
The Power of Prayer

Shortly after I broke up with my boyfriend, I read something in a teen girl's devotional that made an impact on me. The author encouraged young women to be praying for their future husbands. She also shared the beautiful and creative idea of writing letters to your future spouse to present as a gift on your wedding day. I took the advice to heart and began to pray for my future mate. I prayed that God would protect him and his purity. I prayed that if he was not yet a born-again Christian, he would find the Lord quickly. I prayed that God would prepare us for one another. I didn't pray these things on a regular basis, probably only a handful of times, but years later I would discover with wonder that the Lord indeed heard my prayers, and He was faithful to answer!

During this season I also composed a letter to my future husband. I'm not sure what became of that first letter; sadly, it was lost along the way. However, I resumed this practice in college, and on our wedding day, I presented Shawn with a treasure box filled with these letters written just for him, before and after I knew that he was the one. In the very top of the chest I placed my purity ring, the symbol that I had saved my virginity for our wedding night.

******

Meanwhile in Minnesota…

Shawn, who is a few years younger than I, was entering his first year of high school. He still held a lot of anger inside, but he mostly kept it in check. Through an early introduction to pornography, inappropriate movies and the influence of his circle of friends, Shawn had a very impure thought life fantasizing about women. During his freshman year he entered into a dating relationship with a young woman. Though they had not yet become sexually active, they were moving in that direction at a rapid rate. Seemingly out of the blue he began to experience an unexplainable guilt for what he was doing. He realized he was using her, and that it would be wrong to sleep with her. He didn't know where these feelings were coming from. His friends would have only encouraged him to take things as far as he could. However, the guilt was weighing down on him, and he ended the relationship before forfeiting his virginity.

The following summer he was sitting through another church service during which he usually slept. However, this time when the altar call was given he felt compelled to go to the front, but he resisted and stayed in his seat. Afterwards, he felt a deep sorrow in his heart. He told God, "If they have another altar call next week, I will go up." Sure enough the next week he responded and walked to the front of the church. The pastor asked him what he had come for. Shawn suddenly broke and began to weep. All he could say was "I'm a sinner! I'm a sinner!" In the moments that followed, a young man surrendered his life to Jesus Christ and received the free gift of forgiveness and salvation from his sins. He became a new creation!

The changes in Shawn were drastic. His language cleaned up almost immediately. In God's goodness, He touched Shawn's mind in such a way that he no longer struggled with impure thoughts. They just weren't there anymore. He had such a hunger for God's Word and would spend hours reading the Bible. His friends didn't know what to do with him, and he lost many of them. He was not yet connected with other Christian kids at his school, so he spent a lot of time alone those first few months, reading the Bible and getting to know this God Who had so transformed his life. In time he got plugged in with a youth group in town; (his home church was very small and didn't have a youth program). He was learning and growing at a rapid rate as God shaped his mind and desires in a brand new way.

He was interested in a few girls throughout the rest of his high school years and went on a date or two but nothing serious. Somewhere along the way he was introduced to Joshua Harris' second book *Boy Meets Girl*. It was the sequel to *I Kissed Dating Goodbye* and shared the author's story of meeting, courting and eventually marrying his wife. Shawn was deeply impacted by the book, especially by the couple's choice to save their first kiss for their wedding day. He concluded that he would like to do that as well when the time came, but for right now, girls were just a distraction that he didn't have time for. He even announced to his family that he didn't plan to date until he was twenty-five!

******

If you are single with desire to marry in the future, today is a good day to begin praying for your future spouse if you are not already doing so! Pray this with me:

Father, I thank You that You designed the covenant of marriage to be one of strength and beauty and a reflection of Your heart. Right now I give You my desire for marriage and I trust that You have the best in store. I pray for my future spouse. Protect him/her from temptation and compromise. I pray that he/she would know You and walk closely with You. Give him/her the strength to live a lifestyle of purity until You bring us together. Prepare us both, and help us to find our contentment in You. I pray this in Jesus' name.

6
College Days

With a mixture of excitement and fear, I made the eight-hour drive with my mom from Colby, Kansas to Bartlesville, Oklahoma to begin a new season of my life at Bartlesville Wesleyan College, soon to be renamed Oklahoma Wesleyan University. My senior year of high school had ended up being one of more regret as I foolishly allowed a friend to sway me into entering a "casual" dating relationship with a mutual friend during my last semester. I missed the comfort and attention of having a boyfriend and found ways to convince myself that what I was doing was okay, even though deep down I knew it was wrong. My unwise and selfish choice resulted in needless pain for us both. Now, with a newly strengthened resolve in my heart, I committed to the Lord that I would not date anyone my freshman year and invited Him to heal me from this destructive cycle I kept finding myself pulled into.

I adjusted to college well, enjoying the many new friendships I was building as well as my new level of independence as I slowly transitioned from adolescence into young adulthood. Since I had been very shy during my school years, I was determined to be more outgoing in college, realizing that I had a new beginning with a fresh slate. For the first time in my life, I really loved being at school!

One thing I was not prepared for, though, was a campus full of good-looking Christian young men who were friendly and often held the doors open for the young women as we moved in and out of the buildings on campus! They were so much kinder than many of the boys I grew up with. I successfully completed my first year of school without dating anyone, but that didn't stop me from daydreaming and forming emotional attachments to some of my guy friends. I was learning another hard lesson: heartbreak can spring from presumption and unguarded daydreaming, even if a romantic relationship has never materialized. I allowed my mind and emotions to run away with me, even convincing myself that I'd met "the one," only to feel devastated when I realized those feelings were not returned.

The Lord also began a deep process of healing in me during that first year. It started with the strong conviction in my heart that I had to forgive my dad for the years of pain and neglect I had been carrying around inside. As I looked back on my dating relationships in high school, I realized that the boys I had been drawn to carried some of the same struggles that my dad wrestled with as well. Similar unhealthy patterns had been surfacing in those relationships, though I had been blind to it at the time. It was sobering to acknowledge that my lack of forgiveness was keeping me trapped in the very cycles I was determined not to repeat. I began going to the Lord with the pain and anger in my heart and *choosing* to forgive my dad. It was a process, and there were more hurts to come, but a new measure of freedom came into my life as a result. I was finally able to genuinely pray for him, and I was able to experience God's love for me at a new level. It would be a few more years, though, until I would learn that forgiveness is a two-sided coin. Forgiveness is a choice we make that opens the door for God to begin healing our hearts. However, there is often a need for repentance as well when we have made judgments towards another in bitterness. I will touch on these realities in greater depth in a later chapter.

At one point during my freshman year, I had a powerful touch from the Lord while I was waiting before Him in prayer, asking Him to speak to me. As I waited on Him that day in the small prayer room in one of the women's dormitories, a beautiful scene began to paint itself in my mind's eye. I saw Jesus standing behind me with His arms wrapped around me. I felt so sheltered, comforted and loved. As I looked out, I saw several young men passing by. I heard the Lord speak to my heart, "In the past you have always gone out to one of them. When the right one passes by, though, I will welcome him into the embrace we already share." I was blown away by the Lord's tenderness towards me! This promise became an anchor for my heart during the years that followed as well as a compass back to the right path when I discovered that I had strayed.

I also read two incredible books that year that really helped to reshape my mindsets about singleness, romance, and marriage: *Lady in Waiting* by Debby Jones and Jackie Kendall and *Passion and Purity* by Elisabeth Elliott. In my mind, the wisdom they share is priceless. Here are a few gold nuggets from each:

"A career, a marriage, or even motherhood is not enough to totally satisfy you by itself. God knows that you will never be complete until you really understand that you are complete in Jesus…You were not made to complete another, but to *complement.* Completion is Jesus' responsibility and complementing is a woman's privilege."[6]

"Your hope cannot be in some dreamed up future. It must be in the God who knows your past, present, and future, and loves you enough to give you the best."[7]

"Insecurity keeps a woman from experiencing consistent joy even within a relationship because a man cannot provide security, only God can."[8]

"I do know that waiting on God requires the willingness to bear uncertainty, to carry within oneself the unanswered question, lifting the heart to God about it whenever it intrudes upon one's thoughts. It is easy to talk oneself into a decision that has no permanence—easier sometimes than to wait patiently."[9]

"When obedience to God contradicts what I think will give me pleasure, let me ask myself if I love Him. If I can say yes to that question, can't I say yes to pleasing Him? Can't I say yes even if it means sacrifice? A little quiet reflection will remind me that yes to God *always* leads in the end to joy. We can absolutely bank on that."[10]

"My heart was saying, 'Lord, take away this longing, or give me that for which I long.' The Lord was answering, 'I must teach you to long for something better.'"[11]

7
Life-Changing Experiences

My freshman year of college finished well, and that summer I attended an incredible program called The Laborer's Institute (TLI) through a ministry out of Colorado called Kingdom Building Ministries. It was a three-month discipleship program for young adults. We were divided into four teams of roughly twelve people each, with the addition of two team mentors who had been through the program before. Each team also had a staff leader assigned to them. Our first month consisted of discipleship classes during the day and team-building exercises on the weekends. We were learning so much from so many amazing teachers that some rightly described it as "trying to get a drink of water from a fire hydrant!" I was more excited than ever about my Christian walk, and I enjoyed the process of bonding with my teammates. Some of our team-building exercises included a high-ropes course, a white-water rafting camping trip, and a day-long scavenger hunt through Denver. We were having a blast, growing as a team, and growing in our faith. I was loving it!

During the second month of TLI, each team flew overseas for a short-term mission trip. My team was assigned to Thailand. It was both challenging and amazing! Part of the challenge had to do with packing for a month in nothing but a backpack. This was required as we needed to have the ability to quickly gather our things and carry them at a moment's notice. Out of respect for the culture, the women on our team were asked to wear skirts since we would be working in an area that had a large Muslim and Buddhist influence. I quickly learned that what I *think* I need and what I *actually* need are often two different things. I had room to pack three skirts and four shirts, and I bought a few more skirts in Thailand, leaving my old ones behind. All of our clothes had to be hand-washed in tubs and hung to dry, so we were doing laundry every few days. Towels were too bulky for a backpack already filling up with other necessities, and we were warned that the high humidity of the climate would make it difficult for towels to dry anyway. One teammate had the humorous and brilliant idea of packing car shammies as an alternative. They only took a small amount of space, and they dried quickly.

We were staying at a missionary family's building that had two large rooms of bunk-beds on the top floor. Thankfully, they had Western-style toilets (most public places had "squatty-potties") and running water, though no heated water. The hot summer temperatures made the cold showers more bearable! (The night before we flew back to the States we stayed in a hotel close to the airport. I thought I was in the lap of luxury to have a hot shower and a real bath towel!)

Though most of our time was in a city, but we made a few trips to rural villages and stayed overnight. We visited village schools and helped teach English to the children with songs and activities using games and colorful posters we had already prepared. Most importantly, we just loved on the kids. They were so thrilled to have us there, and they were so starved for attention and affection. We were told ahead of time that in their culture, sniffing someone's cheek is like giving a kiss, so they told us to only let girls sniff girls, and boys sniff boys! The children swarmed us, eager to hug us and to sniff our cheeks. It was precious!

At the first school we visited, the guys on our team slept in the school building, but one of the teachers opened her home for the girls. It was so humbling as she offered us the best she had, which was so very little by Western standards. She didn't even stay in her house that night, allowing us full access. Her home was a modest stone building with a small upper floor where we slept. She had laid down mats wall to wall for us to sleep on and any sort of covering she could find of sheets, pieces of fabric, etc…It was the very best she had to give, and she gave it eagerly. She didn't have indoor plumbing. Her bathroom was a stone room with a squatty-potty that had to be manually flushed with a dipper full of water, and a large stone basin full of water for dipper bathes. A drain built into the floor allowed the water to wash away. I realized more than ever how very much I have to be thankful for that I so easily take for granted.

We ministered in the city as well, taking regular walks down to the outdoor food court of a large university. We would buy our dinner (my favorite was chicken and sticky rice), and we would make conversation with the students, most of whom were eager to practice their English. We looked for opportunities to share Jesus' love with them as we built friendships. I have stayed in touch with one young woman in particular all these years later through the gift of internet.

We also took multiple "prayer walks" around the city, quietly praying and asking God to reveal Himself and bring many to salvation. We blessed the city and the people, inviting the Lord to come and make Himself known. Walking through the city was an experience in itself. There were no underground sewers. Instead, open sewage flowed through deep canals on each side of the road, making the stench overpowering at times. Dirty and half-starved stray dogs were everywhere. We were stationed very close to a Buddhist temple, and the monks would often feed the dogs, believing it improved their karma. Speaking of Buddhism, one day we visited a very large temple that was also a tourist attraction, so we were allowed to enter. In one building we were surrounded wall to wall by black and white pictures of prominent Buddhists who were now deceased. Behind each picture was an enclosed shelf containing their ashes. I was suddenly overwhelmed as the reality started to hit me that I was surrounded by faces of people who had died never knowing Jesus. My heart began to break, and I asked the Lord to give me a greater burden for those who do not yet know Him. This will be my lifelong prayer.

The entire trip made a very big impact on me, but I think it was the village children who impacted me the most. Their clothing was dirty and worn, and most of them were so starved for love. I wanted to scoop them up and take them home with me! It was during this time that the seeds were first planted in my heart with the desire to one day adopt a child, especially from overseas. This is a dream that is still very much alive inside of me, and I am confident that there is a day coming when this dream will become a reality!

After returning from Thailand, we had a few days to rest and sleep off some of our jet lag before embarking on the third and final assignment of the program. My team was sent to beautiful Pagosa Springs, Colorado to spend the month working at a youth ministry outreach. The ministry was founded and operated by Bay and Peggy Forrest. Bay Forrest is a retired NBA player who played for the Phoenix Suns in the late 70's. His 6'10" frame made him quite a sight to behold! He and his wife have a heart of love for youth, and he conducted summer basketball camps with evening chapel services filled with upbeat music, drama presentations and engaging speakers, all to share the Gospel and Jesus' love with the teens that attended. During our time there, we hung out with the kids, played games with them, talked with them, and helped with the chapel services, especially with the music and drama presentations. We had an amazing time, and the highlight for me was when we were able to pray with two hurting sisters to accept Jesus into their lives as their Lord and Savior!

The summer concluded with a banquet and graduation ceremony to celebrate the successful completion of The Laborer's Institute. Saying goodbye to my teammates was both painful and surreal. We had shared three months of our lives together and experienced so much in that short window of time. We had truly become like a family, and it was hard to fathom that I might never see some of them again since we came from different places all across the nation. It was the most powerful three months of my life up to that point, and I knew I would never be the same again. After a couple weeks at home, it was time for me to return to college for my sophomore year.

8
Clutching the Old Security Blanket

Making the transition back to school was more difficult than I had anticipated. The summer with TLI had such an impact on me, and I felt like a different person, but I was returning to an environment that was the same. My time at home had been difficult as well. While I was away for the summer, my mom had become involved in a relationship with a man she had dated years before. I was never comfortable around him, and it was very upsetting to learn they were together again. My mom was going through a real crisis of faith during that time, due to some extremely difficult circumstances, and she wasn't even sure if she still believed in God. I had just come out of such an intense summer, and I was more excited about God than ever before. I wanted everyone to be as excited as me, and I had a hard time understanding what was happening in my mom. The changes taking place in both of us created tension in our relationship that continued for the next few years. She married her boyfriend the next year, making the rift between us even greater. (Their marriage ended six years later, and the Lord started drawing her heart back to Him again. Her faith was rekindled, and she came alive in a way I had never seen before! Our relationship was healed and restored as well.)

I returned to college feeling very alone. I missed my teammates. I grieved the change in relationship with my mom. I wanted someone to talk to who would understand. I spent some time with a girl a few years older than me who had previously attended TLI, which helped some, but I still felt so disoriented. Then one day I went to check my e-mail at the campus library and was not at all prepared for what I would find. I had received a short e-mail from my dad, whom I had not seen since the previous Christmas. His message contained a short paragraph which began with "Greetings from Japan!" He went on to tell me that an opportunity had opened for him to move overseas, and he had already re-located. Over the last several years he had developed a fascination with Asian cultures, but I never expected that he would actually move out of the States. I did not know how to begin to process what he was telling me. No warning, no goodbye, no explanation—he was just gone! Waves of sorrow, anger and rejection began sweeping over me. How could he just leave his kids so suddenly without even saying goodbye? Would I ever see him again?

Not knowing what else to do, I made my way up to the campus pastor's office. A loving father of four daughters, he compassionately listened as I talked and cried, and he prayed with me before I left his office. It helped some, but my heart had been ripped open again, and I was in so much pain. I called my mom and told her through my tears what I had just learned. She was completely shocked as well and had the difficult job of breaking the news to my brother who was still living at home. It seemed as though everything was falling apart.

As the end of the fall semester drew near, announcements for the campus Christmas banquet were sent out in the campus mail. It was a formal event when the young women would pull out their prom style dresses and the young men would wear their suits. My best friend and I were planning on just attending with a group of friends, but then we had the impulsive idea of inviting two of our guy friends for a double date. We didn't know either of them really well, but one of them was in some of my classes. He was funny and engaging, but I had no romantic interest in him at that point, though I was pretty sure he had a little crush on me. He knew how to flirt, and his attention made me feel good. Sure enough, the night of the banquet, he made sure that he was paired with me, and he was so charming. He made me feel beautiful and special, and I found myself drinking it all in. I didn't have a clear sense of what his relationship with God was like. He said he was a Christian, but I didn't know the depth of his walk with the Lord.

To make a long story short, I succumbed to the attention and offered him my phone number over the Christmas break. By the time second semester began, we had entered into a dating relationship, and we were both flying high on the emotions of infatuation. He was so romantic and attentive; he knew just the right thing to say, and he adored me. Our relationship took off in a whirlwind, and when I allowed him to kiss me, things only intensified. Four months later we were engaged, though we were only nineteen at the time. We ignored the concerns that our friends and family voiced to us, convinced that we were in love and this was "meant to be." We started talking about making plans to wed over the next Christmas holiday.

In addition, he was a very skillful musician, and he wanted to transfer to a college in his home town that had a bigger music program. As his devoted fiancée, I determined that I would transfer with him, willingly leaving the Christian college I had chosen to attend a secular university I knew nothing about. With emotions high, we moved back to his home town over the summer, where his parents set up a guest room for me to stay. However, as I started looking through wedding magazines and daydreaming about plans, he started hanging out with his old group of friends and acting increasingly detached. His demeanor and language were changing; this wasn't the same guy I had known just a few months before. He was starting to realize that he was too young to get married, and he was terrified to enter into that level of commitment. Over a heart-wrenching two weeks' time, he broke up with me and reconciled with me a handful of times before ending our relationship for good on my 20th birthday. He didn't do this to be spiteful, but while we were out on a date to celebrate, I was grilling him about what in the world had been going on over the last few weeks, and he finally said, "I can't do this anymore. I'm not ready." I was completely devastated.

I returned to Oklahoma Wesleyan University in the fall and was both excited and disheartened when he decided to return as well. It was so painful to see him on campus, which was unavoidable at such a small school. At the same time, I missed him desperately and still clung to the hope that we would reconcile again. I was not willing to admit that it was God's protection for both of us that we didn't go through with marriage. I didn't want to come to terms with the fact that this relationship was never the Lord's idea in the first place, but something I had foolishly rushed into. The pain drove me closer to Jesus' heart, though, and I wrote a lot of poetry during that time as a release for my emotions and as a form of prayer. Slowly, I accepted that the relationship was wrong from the start, and while God was compassionate towards my broken heart, I was experiencing pain He had never intended for me to walk through.

The first poem, written while I was still convinced that I was supposed to marry this young man, was titled "Security." Though my understanding of my circumstances at the time was not accurate, the truth of the Lord's heart for me still clearly resounded through my written words.

Security

My security blanket, ragged, dirty and thin
Still tightly I clutched it under my chin
A sense of warmth it never did give
Yet there was no other way I knew how to live

Tenderly my Jesus beckoned me to let go
I knew that I must, but the surrender was slow
"I have something superior to take its place,"
He said, tightly wrapping me in His embrace

I will grant you security, peace, joy and love
As well as treasures below and treasures above

My heart was complete! His love was so real!
For the very first time, my heart truly could feel
And He whispered a promise I'll always hold dear
"When your prince passes by, he too will draw near"

Secure in my Lord, given wings to fly
And then one happy day, my prince did pass by
Through prayer, fasting, and a heart set on Him
Jesus joyfully welcomed my prince to come in

Our love was beautiful, my heart could only sing
We knew it was real for we were under His wings
I remember the day he asked me to be his wife
We would glorify Jesus all through this life

Then one dreadful day the changes began
His heart and face hardened and he suddenly ran
My tears fell around me, the pain was so great
As my prince left the embrace leaving my heart to break

Jesus, why did this happen? Has this been all wrong?
"My child, just trust Me, and I will make you strong
I know that for now, the end is not in sight
Keep your hand in Mine and we'll walk through this night

I know you are hurt; My heart is hurt too
But please never forget, I will never leave you

I know that you feel you have nothing left to give
But in Me you are complete, and in Me you will live

You are a treasure, a gift costly and pure
And your broken, battered heart I promise to cure
The man who will commit to making you his
Will be utterly amazed at all you have to give

A love will return, all is not lost
He is worth whatever wait, and worth whatever cost
And when your heart and his are ready once more
Your prince will arrive again at the door

My precious child, I do love you so
My plans are much greater than you ever could know
So as you patiently wait, please rest solely in Me
For I will always be your True Security"

9
Poetry of Pain and Praise

I want to share a few of the poems I wrote during my season of heartache to show how the Lord met me in the midst of my pain and confusion. The second poem "Broken" is actually published in my first book, *Reflections from Holland: A New Mother's Journey with Down Syndrome.* Though the circumstances that initially drove me to write that particular poem were very specific, the prayer that emerged from it is life-long, and it resonated in my heart again years later in a completely different season of pain and struggle. My prayer is that these words of vulnerability may resonate in your heart as well, whatever season or circumstances you may be facing.

The Journey

This road twists and turns
With no end in sight
The darkness presses in
Will I be consumed by this night?

My feet are heavy-laden
Questions fill my mind
If only I could see around the next bend
Perhaps the answers I would find

But all I can see in this moment is myself
A weary traveler on this road
Each step is shaky and painful
As I strain to walk beneath this heavy load

I was thrown here in an instant
The enemy mocking me all the way
In fear he robbed me of my gift
Hoping to leave me in dismay

And I have allowed him to press
This heavy burden upon my back
He's broken my heart to pieces
In his vicious and evil attack

But now a warm, loving voice
Whispers gently in my ear

"You never have to let him win
There is nothing for you to fear!"

I'm filled with strength as I remember
He has no power over me
For Jesus broke every single chain
Through His blood on Calvary

Yes, this road is long and dark
And the terrain rough beneath my feet
But my Guide sheds light on every step
His Presence is so very sweet!

He gently lifts the load from me
Placing it on His own strong back
He firmly holds my hand in His
As we continue down this track

The answers are still miles away
but the questions haunt me no more
For my Guide is familiar with every step
He's been down this road before

He knows every twist and every turn
He knows when the night will turn to day
He lovingly speaks as we journey on
And picks me a flower along the way

Even though this dark and winding road

Is so hard and so very long
He grants me a sense of inner peace
That I am where I belong

My Loving Guide is beside me
What better place could I ever be?
And when I become too weak and weary
He never hesitates to carry me

So we press on together
Knowing that treasures are in store
But no treasure will ever compare
To the joy of walking with my Lord!

Broken

My defeated, grieving heart
Eyes stained red with tears
Yet on Your altar of grace
I have chosen to lay down my fears

My dreams I had clutched so tightly
The heart is so deceiving
Thinking I knew the way to walk
I kept myself believing

That the truth I had perceived
Must be the only way
When the true desire of Your heart
Is for me to humbly pray

What I had seen as beauty
You knew could soon be shaken
In love You'll never rest
Until I am completely taken

Into the deepness of Your heart
Where my identity is placed
In the promise of Your Cross
And the fullness of Your grace

My broken pieces belong to You
Do with them as You will
And as You overtake me
In Your peace may I be still

This life is Yours, not mine
You are the Lord of all
Direct my path with every step
And catch me when I fall

Burn away my "self"
Until all is stripped away
May I live in brokenness
Each and every day

For there true beauty resides
Your richness fills my soul
As I step into Your Presence

I know I am made whole

Oh, my precious Jesus
Your face is all I seek
I rejoice that You are strong
Every place that I am weak.

I love to stand before You
I want to live before Your eyes
Guard me from the enemy
Free me from all of his lies

One day I will be with You
I'll gaze into Your face
I ache to feel the fullness
Of that tender, intimate embrace

But until that Day arrives
You are my daily food
Please take my broken pieces
And feed a multitude

So that I may stand before You
Knowing I did not live in vain
You are a Sovereign God
And I surrender to You my pain

That You may form beauty from ashes
And build within me a fire

Spreading out to those around me
As I burn with Your desire

Rest
In the midst of
Jumbled thoughts
Racing emotions
Questions and fears
My heart turns to You
Will You give me rest?

So much I carry inside me
Can I give it all to You?
Will all my weaknesses
My desires, my tears
Be a worthy sacrifice?
I offer myself, Lord

I know Your promises
I know they are pure
Why so often
Do truths in my head
Miss embracing my heart?
Change me, O God

You offer a place of rest
Complete wholeness and health
For this weary, troubled soul
Dismissing all else

I lay down in Your stillness
I am desperate for You!

All that is or was
Or could ever be
Is being firmly held
In Your able hands
You know end from beginning
I rejoice in Your victory!

The madness dims
As You take my hand
My spirit is warmed
My mind is stilled
I enter into Shalom
Thank You, Jesus for Your rest!

<u>A Sweeter Song</u>

The pain had pursued me
Weary day after day
I cried out to my Father
Could He see my dismay?

Heat from refining fire
Created jewels in my heart
But how I longed for the hour
When this suffering would depart

I had often been told

The night is blackest before dawn
When the daylight soon arrives
Your pain will be gone

Jesus, please change my heart
I have hurt for so long
I desire Your perfect will
May I taste a sweeter song?

Then in the stillness of my soul
His healing waters began to flow
Pain and sorrow were washed away
And I began to truly know

That I am a costly treasure
Worth much more than I can see
And my prince whom He's preparing
Is beyond my wildest dreams

He has a sweeter song in store
A love reflecting His lovely face
A man of God to share with me
In the shelter of His warm embrace

A story to be penned in perfect time
For He is the Author of love and romance
The Master Musician will play His song
And my prince and I will begin our dance

Dependence

While the raging fire blazed
And all around me was black as night
I desperately clung to Your side
My soul's sole Source of Light

My weaknesses laid completely bare
Pain engulfed my heart and mind
Yet I knew only in Your embrace
True security would I find

Though the suffering was so intense
Your fellowship tasted so sweet
Each day I longed with anticipation
For our next dear chance to meet

My growing hunger for You
Gave me increasing strength to press on
My heart's desire was to walk with You
As You led me towards the dawn

The brilliant sun is now shining
Through the dense, dark and sorrowful mist
The night is quickly dissolving
At last suffering lowers his fist

I rejoice in this brand new day
My Jesus has blessed me so
Yet I miss the helpless dependence

Only my bitter tears could sow

Jesus, I receive Your outpour of blessings
But I desire most to see Your face
Teach me to live whether rain or shine
In the shelter of Your warm embrace

Whether walking through fire or by peaceful shore
My dependence on You remains the same
May my greatest delight forever be found
In the glory of Your unchanging Name

10
Emotions Can Be Deceiving

While still in the process of healing from my broken engagement, I discovered some new friendships on campus with a few other young women. We spent a great deal of time together, and the laughter and lightheartedness we shared was medicine to my soul. I was enjoying the sense of camaraderie, and I was accepting the fact that I should have never gotten engaged in the first place. I surrendered my heart to the Lord in this area again, praying "I am not good at figuring this whole thing out, and I can't trust my own heart. Please bring the right person into my life at the right time, but please let him be older and more mature!" I prayed that last part partially joking and partially serious. I thought an older guy would be more stable and better prepared for marriage. For now, though, I was going to focus on college, enjoying friends, and growing in my relationship with Christ.

One of my teammates from The Laborer's Institute was getting married in Mississippi over the Thanksgiving holiday that year, and she asked me to be one of her bridesmaids. I was thrilled at the prospect of seeing her again, and I was so honored that she wanted me to be in her wedding! I had a wonderful time while I was down South. The bride's and groom's families were both so loving and welcoming. Her grandmother even offered for me to stay with her should I ever want to come visit for an extended period of time.

During the rehearsal dinner, we were given assigned seats, and I happened to be seated at a table with a few others, including one of the groomsmen. He was a few years older than me, and he definitely fit into the "tall, dark, and handsome" category. I felt a bit nervous in his presence, and I was surprised at his eagerness to make conversation with me, not just at the dinner, but throughout the weekend. His attention was completely unexpected. My self-esteem was not very high, and I would have considered him to be "out of my league." Yet here he was, seeking me out, intent and friendly as we conversed. He was very much a gentleman, and from our conversation, I could tell he loved the Lord. I felt completely swept off my feet when he asked me to dance at the wedding reception. My friend's aunt only added to my heightened emotions when she had us pose together for a picture and kept saying with a grin, "You two just *look* like you go together!" It felt like something out of a storybook. My heart was pounding later when he asked me for my phone number and permission to call me after I returned to Oklahoma. Was this really happening?

This apparent "Prince Charming" wasted no time in contacting me during the following week. We began talking on the phone regularly, often late into the night until we were both too sleepy to stay awake any longer. Since we talked so often, we felt so connected, and it didn't take long before he asked if I would be his girlfriend. I didn't hesitate to say yes, convinced that God had answered my prayer much sooner than I had anticipated. It just *felt* so right. I overlooked the fact that he didn't have clear direction for his life and was working a few random jobs, just trying to make ends meet. Everyone has to start out somewhere, right? He loved God, and he was taken with me. Everything else would work out.

I was so convinced that we were meant to be, that I arranged to spend my summer in Mississippi to fulfill my required internship program for my behavioral science major. My friend's grandma was very willing to let me stay with her in Vicksburg, and I was accepted for an internship at the Vicksburg Family Development Center. However, waiting until summer time to see each other again felt like too long a wait. Our desire to be together only intensified with every phone conversation. One weekend, on a whim, he borrowed a friend's car (his wasn't reliable enough for long distance driving) and made the 8-9 hour drive to Bartlesville after finishing his work shift. In his weariness, he drove right through Bartlesville and hit the Kansas border 20 miles later, having to turn around again. I was a ball of nervous excitement as I waited for him to arrive. We would only have a day together before he would have to make the drive back for work. A handful of girls from campus waited with me outside one of the dormitories. They were eager to see in person this guy I was beaming about all the time. When he finally arrived, he exited the car with a bouquet of roses in his hand and was a bit surprised by the small "audience" that greeted him. I don't remember many details from that day; only that it ended way too soon, and it was time to say goodbye again.

I was very active in the campus theater program, and shortly after his visit I was performing in a musical that I really wanted him to be able to attend. He could not afford another trip to Oklahoma, but I managed to collect enough money to buy him a bus ticket so he could come for the performance. I also arranged for him to stay with my mentor and her husband, a middle-aged couple who lived across the street from campus. He agreed to come, but he was not prepared for what would follow. The bus ride itself was extremely long and taxing, and a day after he arrived, an unexpected blizzard moved into the area, covering the streets with ice and burying the town in snow. All bus routes were cancelled for a few days, and he was stuck following me around campus class to class as he worried about his job back in Mississippi. He could not afford to take all of this time off, and his boss was not happy about the situation. He was concerned he may not have a job when he returned. When the bus station finally opened again, I saw him off, but already his attitude toward me seemed to be different. I reasoned it away, thinking that it was just due to him being tired and stressed.

A few nights later on the phone, he spoke the words I wasn't prepared to hear again, and told me he thought it would be best for us to end the relationship. He said it wasn't fair to me for us to continue in a relationship when he had no real direction for his life yet. He needed to get some clear focus before he pursued a serious relationship. I wondered why he had not considered that before pursuing me in the first place, but, then again, I hadn't considered it either. All I knew was that I was crushed and couldn't believe I was having my heart broken again so soon. I was so sure that this relationship was from the Lord. Why did I keep getting myself into these messes? To make matters worse, I was committed to my internship at this point. How could I face seeing him?

I felt so foolish for planning my whole summer around a relationship that seemed secure but was really just shifting sand. My only consolation was that we had never kissed. We only saw each other a few times, and we were both mindful of maintaining physical purity. Our physical affection had not moved past holding hands, some cuddling, and a light peck on the cheek. At least I hadn't given that part of my heart away again.

I spent the rest of the semester throwing myself head first into hanging out with my friends. I started experimenting with new hairstyles, new fashion, and new music. I had always kind of fit the stereotype of "the girl next door," and I wanted to break out of that mold and try to figure out who I really was. I went about it in completely the wrong way. A few of my friends were more fashionable, outgoing, and spontaneous than I was naturally, and I tried to follow their lead and act more like them. They were Christians, but our interaction with each other was usually more surface level in nature. We were not encouraging each other to draw closer to God. Bit by bit, my relationship with Jesus was becoming dull. I still loved Him, but I wasn't spending the time with Him that I used to, and the more time I spent pursuing things that were shallow and entertaining, the more distant I felt from Him. I started watching movies that a year prior I would not have been comfortable viewing, and I started listening to music that I wouldn't have been comfortable listening to before. I was searching for identity, trying to prove something, but not sure what I was trying to prove. I was starting to feel empty inside, even though I was enjoying myself. I was still hurting too, and the constant activity and entertainment helped to numb the pain. One day I found myself alone in the "prayer tower" of one of the girl's dormitories as I penned the following poem:

Renewal

I run all day trying to fill this hole
I fear the silence telling me I have no control
Wonderful friends fill my days with laughter
Yet I question what it is that I'm running after

Who am I? Do I really know?
So much inside me that is waiting to grow
So many questions with no answers in sight
I feel so small and consumed with fright

I want to become who You created me to be
I want to truly feel that my spirit is free
But today a heaviness weighs on my heart
A cloud has descended, chilling every part

Where is the victorious life You promise to give?
Why do I hold hurt when You've called me to live?

Why is my spirit so full of unrest?
Why can't I remember that You truly know best?

Why do I allow pride to block fellowship with You?
Why don't I allow my Father to make me new?
I feel so let down by the world I am in
Help me to remember that I am born again

I want a man to love me
To cherish me in his soul
Why do I forget in You
I'm cherished and made whole?

Why do I keep running
When You've asked me to be still?
Why am I always fighting
Between my spirit, flesh and will?

Please break me once again
Lay me down upon my face
Be for me a refuge
My only resting place

I need You, my Sovereign Lord
I'm crying out to You
Wrap me in Your embrace
And show me what to do

Teach me who I am

The woman You created
May I live a life sold out to You
A life to be celebrated!

But for now just hold me close
And whisper Your love in my ear
Promise that You'll never leave
Tell me I have nothing to fear

I'm a child missing her Daddy
Needing His gentle touch
With my head on Your chest I hear every heartbeat,
And I know that You love me this much

So as I snuggle closely to Your side
Though my tears begin to pool
I know in You is found my hope
My strength and my renewal

11
Paths Prepared to Meet

Though the circumstances were not what I once envisioned, my summer in Mississippi ended up being a very beneficial one, full of new experiences and opportunities to grow. As promised, my friend's grandmother graciously opened her home to me for the summer. I saw my ex-boyfriend a few times during those three months, and we were able to find some resolution and closure for our relationship in a way that was healing for us both. My internship with The Vicksburg Family Development Center was a Godsend. Though it was not a Christian organization, every single employee was a Christian, and it was directed by two very kind and godly women. Our weekly staff meetings included a prayer time at the end. I was busy working with teenagers, pre-school age children (my favorite), and I even filled in for the secretary for a time while she was out on medical leave. I also had the opportunity to take a few weeks off from my internship to be a camp counselor at a Christian camp in Georgia that my friend was involved in each year. It was a very rewarding experience!

My most unique opportunity, however, opened up one day when I brought my guitar by the office. I had only been playing for less than a year, and I did not have any formal training. A friend at college had showed me some basic chords, and I muddled my way through. I have always loved to sing, and I was able to play some simple worship songs. One of my directors, named Linda, ministered at a small African American church in town. She invited me to come play my guitar one Sunday, and ended up inviting me to be their worship leader for the duration of the summer. They had a small children's choir but no worship leader. I wasn't much of a guitar player, but I could get by, and I was honored by the offer. I couldn't help but find the humor in the scenario, however. Here I was, a little white girl from rural Kansas, leading worship at a southern African American church! Only God can bring things like that together. I loved my time there. The people began to feel like family, and Linda was a mentor to me, helping me to grow deeper in my walk with God. I will forever be grateful to her!

Meanwhile in Minnesota...

As I was in the midst of my junior year of college, Shawn was finishing his senior year of high school. He still wasn't sure what he wanted to do after graduation, and he was kind of dragging his feet about looking into colleges. His family assumed he would opt to attend a state school, and he already had several credit hours completed from a local university by attending concurrent classes during his last two years of high school. At age sixteen, he had been sure that he was going to join the military and even tried to enroll, only to find out that he had to be seventeen. In that year of waiting, God began to shift things in his heart, and he realized that he really wanted to be involved in ministry of some sort, though he didn't know in what capacity.

He had developed a growing interest in the international persecuted church after reading the book *Jesus Freaks,* which was a compilation of historical and present-day stories of Christian martyrs. He also read *Tortured for Christ*, the story of Romanian pastor Richard Wurmbrand, who suffered greatly under the Russian communist regime and later founded the international ministry The Voice of the Martyrs (VOM) after escaping to the United States with his family. Shawn was gripped by the genuineness and boldness of the faith of those he read about. He started receiving VOM's monthly newsletter and devoured each issue. VOM is an international ministry to persecuted Christians throughout the nations of the earth, offering various forms of aid and intervention, smuggling the Bible into closed nations, and being a voice to create awareness to the outside world about the plight of many Christians today. Amazingly, the headquarters for this global ministry is located in none other than Bartlesville, Oklahoma.

As Shawn was reading the newsletter one day, he saw an advertisement for a brand new endeavor by VOM as they partnered with Oklahoma Wesleyan University to develop a unique major called "Ministry to the Persecuted Church." Something inside of him jumped, and he knew that was where he wanted to be. OWU was the only school he applied to, and he excitedly announced to his family that he was planning to move down to Oklahoma to attend college. They were shocked and somewhat dismayed at his choice, hoping he would remain close to home, but he was a determined young man. He was accepted to the university and made plans to attend for the fall semester.

Incredibly, he was actually accepted on human error, though we know it was divinely planned. He somehow neglected to take his ACT test, and the university never asked for his score. It was only after arriving on campus and meeting with the financial aid department that it was discovered that the school had accepted him as a transfer student, believing he had already completed a year of college due to his multiple credits earned while still in high school. Since he was already there and enrolled in classes, they graciously allowed him to stay!

******

As my summer in Mississippi was starting to wrap up, I had an unexpected wave of grief over my broken engagement resurface. It caught me completely off-guard, since I sincerely believed that I had fully moved on. I didn't tell anyone what I was experiencing, but one morning at church I went up with a group of people after an invitation from Linda to receive prayer. Without me saying a word to her, she started declaring to me, "There have been some hurts from your past that have been re-surfacing and hurting you again like they did when they first happened, but God wants you to know that it's because He's healing you, and you are about to enter into a brand new season." I was completely blown away!

On a different day I was praying in the car on my way to our weekly staff meeting, and I was suddenly hit with a deep ache to meet my future husband. I was surprised by this surge of unexpected emotion. I desired to follow the path that God had for me presently, even if that meant an extended season of singleness. I talked to God about what I was feeling, offering it back to Him. At the end of the staff meeting, people were giving prayer requests, and I shared something completely unrelated to my experience in the car. I don't remember now exactly what it was for, but I know it had nothing to do with relationships. Linda came and prayed over me, and I was shocked again as she started to pray at one point that the Lord would prepare my future husband and me for each other and that He would allow our paths to cross soon! It was actually a little embarrassing in the context of a staff meeting, but I was encouraged, realizing that the Lord wanted to remind me again that my heart matters to Him. I told Linda later about what happened while I was driving to work, and she was very relieved. She felt funny praying about my future husband, since it seemed out of context and unrelated, but she felt such a strong impression from the Lord that she was supposed to pray for me along those lines. I felt so loved!

Soon it was nearly time to return to Oklahoma for my senior year, and I was pleased that I had room in my schedule to take one of the introductory classes for the new Ministry to the Persecuted Church program. I had also read *Jesus Freaks* as a teenager, and I was intrigued by this new program. I was optimistic about my last year of college, wondering what God had planned for my future. One thing was clear, though; I wanted *Him* to be the one to chart my course, not my own emotions and seemingly good ideas. I had no way of knowing what He had in store…

12
You Could Marry Him Someday!

I was excited and eager to return to school, happy to reconnect with my friends and ready to enjoy my senior year. As usual, there were several new faces on campus as we welcomed the in-coming class of freshmen. There was one particular freshman named Shawn Hemminger, and I met him on a couple of occasions at the beginning of the semester. We also had one class together, which was the introductory course for the persecuted church ministry major. I recognized that he seemed like a very nice and genuine young man, but he was a freshman, and definitely not on my screen for any sort of romantic interest. As it was, I just wanted to focus on completing school and stepping into the next thing God had for me. I did feel a strange sense of familiarity when I was around him, however, almost like I somehow knew him already. It was a dynamic difficult to articulate, especially since I could not recall having experienced anything like it before.

One day early in the semester, we happened to be seated next to each other in class. While taking notes, he leaned over and asked me how to spell a word, (I wish I could remember what), that I was surprised he didn't know. It was a simple word that I thought any college student should be able to spell, and admittedly I was a bit critical in my mind of his poor spelling skills. However, at the same moment that my thoughts turned critical, a phrase suddenly ran through my mind, crystal clear, and caught me completely off-guard: *You could marry him someday.* What?! Where in the *world* did that come from? Still perplexed, I tried to focus my attention back on class, trying to dismiss such a random and unpremeditated thought. It would only be later that I would discover that Shawn's initial assessment of me when we first met was that, though friendly, I was a bit of a ditz. He happened to run into me with my best girlfriend while we were in a very goofy, hyper mood after recently reuniting from a summer apart. It wouldn't be long, though, before both of our opinions would begin to change…

13
Chocolate Chip Cookies

There came a day after class that both Shawn and I needed to speak with the professor. That same week OWU was hosting a guest speaker from The Laborer's Institute (TLI), the same ministry program I had attended a few years prior. During one of the chapel services he requested that any students who had been a part of TLI would stand up. Shawn noticed me stand and concluded that I couldn't be a complete ditz if I had gone on a mission trip before! This simple event sparked conversation between us after class as we both finished speaking with our professor and headed back across campus toward the cafeteria. I was surprised by the easy flow of dialogue between us. He was very interested to learn more about TLI, and I encouraged him to come to a small informational meeting to be held that night before the chapel service. I would be there with other graduates of the program to answer questions and share some of our experiences. He happily agreed to attend.

The meeting that night went smoothly, and we enjoyed another dynamic chapel service with the guest speaker, who was so energetic, funny, and spiritually stirring. Afterward, Shawn and I ran into each other again down at the campus center. He was excited about what he had learned about TLI and continued to ask me more questions. I told him that I had a scrapbook video from my summer there, full of pictures and testimonies from all members of my team. He surprised me by responding, "Can we watch it now?"

Shortly after, we gathered with a few other students in the lounge area of one of the girls' dormitories, and I popped in the tape. (Yes, we still used VHS some in those days!) Now, before I get any further into the events of that evening, I need to give some background information about a specific story that the TLI speaker had shared previously that week. He enthusiastically told us about his first encounter, as a college student, with his wife years before. He noticed a pretty girl in one of the campus buildings one day who looked very downcast. In his outgoing and unabashed way, he smiled at her, patted her shoulder, and tried to cheer her up sharing, "God loves you!" Hours later upon returning to his dorm, his football buddies grilled him, "Who is she?!" He had no idea what they were talking about until he noticed a plateful of homemade chocolate chip cookies and a card with his name on it. After devouring several cookies he opened the card to find a note of thanks from a young woman who had desperately needed encouragement that day. He didn't recognize her name, so he pulled out a year book and recognized her to be the same pretty girl he had spoken to earlier. The rest was history!

After completing the scrapbook video that night, Shawn, I, and another guy friend of mine stood around outside chatting. Seemingly out of the blue Shawn suddenly turned to me and asked, "Do you know how to make chocolate chip cookies?" There was a moment of awkward silence as I thought to myself, "Is this freshman trying to hit on me?" I don't remember exactly how I responded, but conversation moved on and we soon parted ways for the evening. The next morning I told the speaker what had happened. He just smiled and said, "I'm not saying anything!" It wouldn't be until months later that I would learn that Shawn was not thinking about the chocolate chip cookie story at all when he asked his strange question. Instead, his mind had wandered back to a conversation that he had with a guidance counselor who was giving him a tour of the campus before the semester started. He had encouraged Shawn to look into forming study groups for some of his classes, and he added the advice, "Make sure you invite some girls who know how to make chocolate chip cookies!" It seems that Shawn thought I could be a good candidate for this. While the study groups with cookies never materialized, something was put into motion that night that would change both of our lives forever.

14
A Season for Love?

After the evening discussing The Laborer's Institute, it seemed that Shawn and I continually ran into each on campus. With each encounter, conversation flowed easily, and we were enjoying each other's company. We also had some mutual friends, so we often found ourselves in many of the same group settings. I felt an increasing pull to be around this young man, but I tried to reason it away. He was only a freshman. I was a senior. I had prayed for someone older. I didn't want to get entangled in a relationship again that wasn't in God's plan for me. Besides, Shawn had communicated that he wasn't interested in dating anyone at this time. He didn't say this as a direct comment towards me, but it had somehow surfaced in conversations.

In time, though, our "chance" encounters were becoming more "planned" encounters. We would meet up in the campus center, eat with friends in the cafeteria, and then take long walks around the campus or in one of the neighborhoods close by. We would go to the local bookstore with our friends to study, hang-out, and drink the $0.25 coffee they had available, but would inevitably gravitate toward one another during the outing. On one particular evening at the bookstore, Shawn made a comment in the midst of a group conversation that definitely got my attention. As I have mentioned earlier, I was deeply impacted by Joshua Harris' books on relationships as a teenager. I was touched and challenged when I read that he and his wife had decided to save their first kiss for their wedding day, but I had mostly given up on such a notion. How many guys out there would be willing to make that radical of a commitment? Did I even have the strength for that kind of commitment? The conversation that night must have somehow shifted to relationships because Shawn interjected, "The next girl I date might not be too happy with me because I don't want to kiss until my wedding day." There was a bit of an awkward silence from the group before things moved on. However, inside I was exclaiming, "Oh my goodness, guys like Joshua Harris really do exist!"

Over the next few months, Shawn and I were quickly becoming the best of friends. People on campus would question if we were a couple, and we would assure them that we were "just friends," but everyone else, our professor included, was keenly observing the romance that was developing. I felt so safe with Shawn. He was one of the most genuine people I had ever met. It seemed he didn't even know how to be anyone but himself. I never felt that he was trying to impress me or that he had any ulterior motives. On the contrary, he had quite the knack for putting his foot in his mouth and was getting to be fairly well-known for it around campus! Since he was so innocent, though, it was usually more humorous than offensive.

My favorite story along this line happened one morning in the cafeteria during breakfast. We were sitting with a group of friends when someone spilled their orange juice. Shawn quickly ran off to get a towel, but we were able to take care of the mess with napkins before he got back. Since he was holding a dry towel, he decided to be ornery with it and playfully whacked me in the shoulder. A few moments later, he hit the towel into his open palm, but the movement caused me to flinch. Apparently, my sudden motion stirred up memories of his German Shepherd at home who would occasionally cower when he was going pet her if she had just recently been disciplined for something. Without using a filter (or common sense), Shawn suddenly declared, "I hate it when my dog shies away from me when she thinks

I'm going to hit her!" Our friends immediately exclaimed, "Shawn! Did you just call Dana a dog?!" As the reality of what he had just done quickly set in, Shawn started scrambling for words, trying to explain himself, as he awkwardly said, "No, no, no; it just *reminded* me of my dog." Realizing that he was only digging his hole deeper, he decided to go the extra mile. Turning to me he smiled and said, "If it makes you feel any better, my dog's pretty!" As we left the cafeteria that day, he suddenly got down on his knees and in front of me, while he playfully and dramatically begged for my forgiveness. Who could be mad at that?!

It was during this time that we went on our first "date." The campus hosted an event called "Create-A-Date." To participate, two guys and two girls were to pair up with only $10 and three hours to enjoy the most creative double date they could come up with. At the end of the evening, everyone met in the cafeteria and each team had a few minutes to share their evening's adventures. A panel of student judges picked first through third place winners and prizes were awarded. Shawn and I decided to team up with another guy and girl who were in a similar season of friendship. *(Incidentally, they got married within the same year that we did!)* We put our heads together and decided to go the "wacky" route instead of trying to come up with something romantic. After all, we were all just friends.

Our first stop was at the local dollar store where we purchased water color paints, paper, water balloons and a plastic bat. We then headed to the grocery store to pick up some pre-packaged cookie dough before returning to campus. We made use of the kitchen area in the lobby of one of the women's dorms for the next phase of our date. While the other two got busy baking cookies and filling water balloons, Shawn and I created water color thank you cards for the local police department. With our freshly dried cards and freshly baked cookies, we then drove to the police department. The officers on duty weren't sure what to make of this team of hyper college students offering them our original art work, but they had no complaints about the cookies. As we enthusiastically shared our story, one good-natured and funny officer just looked at us and then pretended he was smoking a joint! Before leaving, we snapped a picture of him hand-cuffing Shawn and me together. *(We ran into this same man awhile back as we were taking our children for a walk in their stroller. I told him, "This is all your fault. Since you hand-cuffed us that night we decided to be joined for life!" He got a good laugh out of that one!)*

After making our delivery we headed downtown with our plastic bat and balloons and enjoyed a game of water balloon baseball with the goal of giving our date a good soaking! Wet, laughing, and having more time to kill, we decided to spend our last dollar for the evening at McDonalds. We ordered a Hot Fudge Sunday from the value menu and split it four ways. We got some stares snapping pictures in the indoor play area and then headed outside. We spread a blanket on the grass and each painted a water-color portrait of our date under the glow of the golden arches. Our three hours completed, we headed back to campus, excited to share about our fun-filled evening. We didn't win any awards that night, but we definitely made some great memories!

As our friendship grew, so did my affection for Shawn. I was alarmed by what I was feeling. I certainly did not trust my own heart after my history of relational shipwrecks. One evening in my dorm room, I penned the following poem as a prayer:

Seasons

You have seen me through so much
Through laughter, tears, joy and pain
My heart broken countless times
The pieces surrendered to You again

Your love has strengthened and healed my wounds
Leaving only scars to testify
In Your embrace true life is found
Though in the process my self must die

You've promised to guard this heart of mine

To hold me secure to the end
Saving me for the man who will be
A reflection of You, my Lover and Friend

So many times I've believed he had come
My deceitful heart clouding the sight of Your will
Once more I feel strongly drawn to another
Could this be the one or another imposter still?

He's committed to guarding my heart and his
Remembering he's my brother
Spurring me closer to You
But my affection for him grows stronger each day
Lord Jesus, give me wisdom; show me what to do!

I know he cares for me as I care for him
But this is not the season for a love to be in bloom
Our friendship still a bud must be watered, nurtured, tended
Until within our hearts commitment is given room

And should this friendship never grow to be
A life-long partnership to glorify You
Keep us both in Your perfect peace
As our hearts remain steadily focused on You

But if a love is to be formed
Guide us each step along the way
Cast out fear that may hinder our union

May You be the Potter and we the clay

Soon after, I went out to a coffee shop one evening with a close girl friend of mine and poured out my heart to her. I cried as I told her, "I think I'm falling in love with Shawn. I don't know what to do! We've gotten so close, and my heart is so attached. He's just starting college. I don't want to be a distraction to him. I don't know if this is God's will or not." She listened and gave me the wise advice, "You two really need to sit down and have a heart-to-heart about all of this. You need to define your relationship."

Later that night, Shawn and I sat together in a large classroom in the upper floor of the campus sports center. I nervously told him that I needed him to decide what his intentions were towards me. I told him that my heart was getting too involved and that if it wasn't his desire to pursue a relationship with me, we needed to take some major steps back. I needed to guard my heart. I fully expected him to say that we should step back in our friendship and the amount of time we spent together. I was already hurting inside at the prospect, but, from my understanding, he did not want to be romantically involved with anyone at that time. Instead he surprised me by responding, "May I have your mom's phone number? I want to call her tomorrow and ask for her permission to court you." (We used the term "courtship" because we were intentionally pursuing the prospect of marriage, not simply dating for the sake of dating). I couldn't believe what I was hearing. We parted ways that night both feeling a bit surreal. Had we really just taken our friendship to the next level? What was this supposed to look like now?

15
Testing the Boundaries

Over the next few days, Shawn and I both felt like we were in a bit of limbo. We knew we cared for each other deeply, and we had been very comfortable in our interaction as friends, but there was uncertainty of how things would be different now that we were officially a "couple." Should things look different? We were committed to physical purity, and we made the mutual agreement that we would wait to kiss, but what should our physical boundaries be? As best friends, we had given each other hugs or occasionally put an arm around the other. Were we to continue on the same just knowing that now we were intentionally pursuing something deeper? In hindsight it seems a bit silly, but there was definitely some confusion starting out. I have to laugh at some of it now. During our first week of courting, we went for a walk downtown, and I took his arm. Shawn suddenly moved my arm and then placed my hand in his. We walked like that for a few minutes, enjoying the new sensation, but we must have been nervous because our palms got so sweaty it didn't last long!

We desired accountability in our relationship, and we soon befriended a middle-aged couple and their family, who spoke into our individual lives and our relationship for the next few years. We were able to glean from their wisdom and gain some new perspectives when needed. Though we didn't always agree with everything they shared, we took their counsel to heart, and we learned a lot more about God and ourselves during that season. I would highly encourage any couples seriously considering marriage to find trusted adults who can offer accountability and advice.

We began courting near the beginning of November, and before we knew it, Christmas vacation was quickly approaching. Shawn asked his mom if he could bring Dana home for Christmas break, and she agreed. With my mom's blessing I happily accepted the invitation. Before we actually left on our trip though, Shawn was talking with his mom on the phone and mentioned his girlfriend. She was shocked. "Dana's your girlfriend?! I thought you were bringing home a guy friend!" (Dana *can* be a male name, though it's not as common.) I was shocked too, wondering how platonically he had spoken about me up to that point! Thankfully, she was still willing for me to come and had prepared a guest room. The news that Shawn actually had a girlfriend and that she would be coming to visit travelled quickly through his Minnesota family and friends. After all, he had announced that girls were a distraction, and he didn't plan to date until he was twenty-five! They couldn't wait to meet this girl from college, especially an older girl. How did he manage that?

We made the long drive up north with a fellow classmate who lived in a neighboring city. I was becoming increasingly nervous as the time actually approached for me to meet his family. What would they think of me? Would we get along well? We had an entire month off from college to spend with them. Shawn kept assuring me not to worry, and he was more than right. His family welcomed me with open arms, and I was able to experience something I had always wanted--a big family Christmas--three of them to be exact. We celebrated with his mom's family, his dad's family, and his stepdad's family. Each gathering was unique and enjoyable, and I received a warm welcome at each one. His mom and I especially connected and had a great time together. I couldn't get over how youthful she was, only sixteen years my senior, and she looked younger than her age. I fell in love with his whole family, and by the time we were finally ready to head back to Oklahoma, I was even more hopeful of marrying Shawn one day!

However, the long break tested the physical boundaries we had initially set in place. We had never been able to spend this much time together, including all the evening time. Sometimes we were alone at night, when defenses are generally down. We found ourselves snuggling up on the living room furniture more and more, at times closer to lying than sitting. One particular evening we were in the basement den by ourselves. We were both tired and started cuddling. Shawn's hand found my leg, and he started gently rubbing. I knew in the back of my mind that we were taking things further than we wanted to, but I wasn't feeling a very strong resolve at that point. Thankfully, a minute later he pulled back and said, "We need to stop." He went on to tell me that he had been silently praying that God would help us to stay pure, when he clearly heard the Lord say back to him, "Then stop doing what you're doing!" It was a much needed wake-up call for us both. We had been courting less than two months, and we were already quickly pushing past the boundaries we had agreed to in our relationship. We realized it wasn't enough to have good intentions. We needed to make deliberate choices about when and where we would allow ourselves to be alone, and we needed more than our own will-power to sustain us. Thankfully, as we prayed, God's grace poured in, and we were able to step back without much of a struggle from that point forward.

16
Purity: The Heart of the Matter

I want to take a break from our story at this point to discuss the heart of this book: purity. I realize that many will not understand or agree with Shawn's and my decision to save our first kiss for marriage, and that's okay. Some may see our choice as extreme or even legalistic. Others may feel inspired and desire to do the same. There is not a universal right or wrong choice in this matter. For Shawn and me, this was the right choice for us. I am not advocating that everyone must approach their dating relationships the way that we did, but I will say with confidence that I have never regretted our decision, even for a moment!

I remember reading an article on sexual purity in a Christian teen magazine when I was in high school. It was very convicting to me at the time. The writer used the image of a dot in the middle of a large circle to address the commonly asked question, "How far is too far?" The dot was to represent both sexual purity and having a close relationship to Christ. Anything outside of the large circle represented the loss of virginity. The point was made that trying to get as close to the outer boundaries of the circle and still be "pure" was the wrong perspective all together. Instead, the question should be, "How close can I get to the center dot? How close can I get to Jesus?" (Words and phrases in quotations are my own.)

Purity truly begins in the heart. Purity is not a set of do's and don'ts. It is not a list of strict rules to be followed. Joshua Harris says it well: "True purity…is a direction, a persistent, determined pursuit of righteousness. This direction starts in the heart, and we express it in a lifestyle that flees opportunities for compromise…"[12] Purity is a heart attitude that desires to give honor: to God, others, and self. The desire for genuine purity is always rooted in love. I love God, and therefore, I do not want to do anything that would create distance in my relationship with Him. I love the person I am dating, and I want to respect and protect him, realizing that unless we enter into the covenant of marriage, he does not belong to me, and I do not belong to him. I love myself, and I recognize that my affections and my body are a valuable gift to be enjoyed and cherished by the one who will commit to me for life. True purity realizes that genuine unmarried love is given tangible expression, not in yielding to the passion and desire of the moment, but in practicing self-control. It realizes that it is not saying "no" to something good but is saying "yes" to something better. The covenant of marriage opens the door for the full expression and fulfillment of passion and desire, without shame or regret. To quote from the book *Lady in Waiting*, "God intended for you to enjoy the fulfillment and pleasure of sex within marriage only. The wonder and joy of this intimate act is maximized through purity before marriage…"[13]

Most importantly, **true purity is not just a desire for morality; it is a desire for a Person**. In His famous Sermon on the Mount Jesus states, *"Blessed are the pure in heart, for they shall see God"* (Matthew 5:8). Purity of heart is only possible through an intimate relationship with Jesus Christ, the Source of our purity and our righteousness. Loving Him and knowing His love is both the highest calling of mankind and the greatest source of pleasure and fulfillment we will ever know. Drawing closer to His heart must be our primary goal if we are going live true lifestyles of purity.

17
Surrender

My last semester of college went by quickly, and Shawn and I continued to deepen our relationship. Our love for one another and our friendship was growing, and I was becoming convinced in my heart that this was truly the man I would marry one day. Though it may have been a little premature, I wrote the following poem for him on February 28, 2004. (Little did either of us know that this would be the same day our daughter Joelle would be born nine years later!)

Promise
The Lord is so careful
With the children He loves
He knows every heart's desire

So He tenderly molds
Painstakingly refines
Consuming our hearts with His fire

His music of love,
Sweet melodies divine
Echo deep in the recesses of my soul

Striking chords of my dreams
Mere words cannot fathom
For in Him all things are made whole

He promised a prince
A man seeking His heart
To share in this love that is true

His peace has descended
Our hearts have been joined
For I know He could mean only you!

Soon it was time for me to graduate, and the family that had been mentoring us graciously allowed me to move in with them for several months as I got my footing and prepared to live on my own. Shawn decided to return home to Minnesota that summer to be with his family. I understood his decision, but it was difficult nonetheless. I was able to fly out and see him once over the summer, but otherwise we were limited to phone calls which were often cut short by a group of eager children from the family who also wanted to talk with him. I missed him so much and couldn't wait for the school year to begin again.

Shawn's return to Oklahoma greeted us with many new transitions. I was now working full-time and no longer on campus while he was busy with his sophomore year of classes. The majority of our time together was spent with the family I was staying with, and our one-on-one time was very limited. This was positive in the sense that there was little to no temptation to push any physical boundaries, but at the same time, we were losing some of the relational intimacy we had developed over the previous year, and I could feel it taking its toll. When I eventually moved into my own apartment with a roommate, we took a long walk together one evening, and we both realized how much we had missed the times we had for just the two of us. We continued to spend a lot of time in group settings, but we also spent time alone at my apartment. (My roommate had family in town, and she was often visiting with them.) In hindsight, I don't think this was a wise idea. I had a large window in my living room, and we always kept it open and tried to stay within its view as a check and balance for our physical affection. However, being alone, especially in the evenings, created needless temptation, and it could very well have looked questionable to others. By God's grace, though, we maintained our boundaries.

As the months continued to slip by, I started to wonder where we were actually headed in our relationship. We had already been courting for well over a year, and I was sure that this was the man I wanted to marry. However, Shawn seemed to be very content with the status quo. We weren't growing apart, but we also didn't seem to be moving forward. One night we attended a Christian meeting at a local church. The guest minister prayed over a young dating couple at one point, blessing their relationship and speaking to them about the purpose and calling of God he saw on their lives. My heart ached for the same affirmation over our relationship.

As I drove Shawn back to campus that night, our relationship became the focus of our conversation, and we continued to talk for a long time in the parking lot after we arrived. I directly asked Shawn what his intentions were at this point. I reminded him that we had entered into our courtship in the first place in order to test the prospect of marriage, but it seemed we were in a holding pattern, not really going anywhere. I did not want to date for the sake of dating. I wanted to be in a relationship that had purpose, but he seemed so content to just continue on as we were indefinitely. He awkwardly responded, speaking words that cut me to the heart. He told me that he cared for me greatly, but he still wasn't sure if this was God's will or not. Feeling hurt and angry, I asked him why he had been with me for a year and a half already if he wasn't sure that I was the woman he wanted to marry?! Nothing was resolved that evening, and we parted ways, unsure if we were still a couple or not. The moment I stepped back into my apartment, my roommate took one look at my face and asked, "What's wrong?" I immediately burst into tears and told her the whole story. It was one of the longest nights of my life.

The next day at work was just as long. At some point Shawn and I made contact with each other, and I went to see him on campus at the end of the day. Both feeling unsure, we sat down on a bench with more distance between us than normal. He told me that the one thing he was sure of was that he didn't want our relationship to end. I communicated the same, and we both felt a wave of relief that we were still together.

In the days that followed, the Lord really began to convict my heart about the control I had placed over my relationship with Shawn. I wanted to marry him so much that I was clinging to him with a closed fist instead of holding him open-handed to God. I couldn't bear the thought that I may have once again given so much of my heart and my time to another guy who was not going to be my husband. I loved Shawn deeply, and the thought of him not being in my life was devastating to consider. However, as I drove across town alone in my car one afternoon, I placed the man I loved and the marriage I desired on the altar of my heart before the Lord. I remember the exact spot I was on the road with a Sonic drive-thru on my right and a gas station on my left. As the tears streamed down my cheeks I prayed, "Jesus, You know how much I love Shawn and how I long to be his wife, *but I want You more.* If this relationship is not Your will for us, and if it will not bring You glory, then please end it today. I don't want to be in anything that You are not a part of. I want Your will for my life, even if that means letting Shawn go forever." Though, everything inside was screaming with this painful surrender, a wave of peace washed over me, and I reminded myself that God always has my very best interest at heart. He was trustworthy, no matter what the outcome would be.

18
You're Going To Chase Me Now!

The afternoon that I released Shawn to the Lord taught me the incredible power of surrender. When I let go there was an immediate shift in our relationship. I never spoke a word to him about the incident, but something had been released spiritually that had tangible results. Shawn suddenly carried a freedom and confidence in his heart towards me that had not been present before. Also, within the next few weeks we had multiple people speak into our relationship and pray over us as a couple. The affirmation I had been longing for was being poured out in abundance, and there was clarity and momentum in our courtship in a way that had never been present before. Soon our conversations were turning more and more to marriage.

Admittedly, we did things a little backwards than the traditional means of engagement. We were both now convinced that it was God's will for us to marry, and we even felt like He was giving us a date for December 18 of that year. However, Shawn still hadn't officially proposed to me! Summer was underway, and he was working full-time on campus and living in the dorms for a very low summer rate. I was the one with a vehicle, and he ate several of his meals with me, so his living costs were minimal. Little did I know that he was saving every penny he could to buy me the nicest ring possible. I would later learn that there was a woman who worked on campus who used to be a jeweler by trade. She no longer worked in that business, but she maintained her license, which gave her the ability to order jewelry directly from the companies, cutting out all of the middle man costs. One thing she loved to do was help young men on campus order beautiful rings for their brides to be. (On our small Christian campus, engagements were popping up left and right!)

One evening in August, Shawn and I had planned a dinner date. I went to pick him up from work, and I couldn't help but wonder if this was the day he would officially propose to me. He seemed distracted and a bit anxious, increasing my suspicion all the more. After enjoying a nice meal together he quickly excused himself, and I was sure that he was going to return with a surprise and a ring. However, nothing happened, and I was feeling disappointed. I would later learn that Shawn did have the ring and was extremely eager to give it to me. However, in his excitement over receiving it, he never actually planned how he would propose, so he was flying by the seat of his pants! When he excused himself, he was trying to reach a friend and have them pick up some flowers for him and deliver them to the restaurant, but he wasn't having any luck.

Following dinner we took a walk through downtown Bartlesville, which hosts some beautiful shallow pools and fountains. We were both distracted; I was wondering if he was going to propose, and he was trying to figure out how to propose. As a result, we talked very little. Shawn suddenly had the idea that it would be fun to get me to chase him around the fountain and then stop as though he found something in the water. He would then present me with the engagement ring. In his excitement, though, he did not consider how to actually get me to chase him. He just randomly turned to me and exclaimed, "You're going to chase me now!" I looked at him a bit bewildered and responded, "No I'm not!" (We just ate, and I had no desire to run). His second plan foiled, he quickly tried to come up with a third. Close by, there was a brick gazebo with a base and ledge that curved out into the shallow pool of the main fountain. He asked me to walk around the ledge with him, and he planned to pretend, once again, that he found something in the water. I thought that his request to walk around the narrow ledge was bizarre, and when I noticed ants crawling on the brick wall of the gazebo, I wanted nothing to do with it. Poor Shawn! He was so excited, and so sincere, but romance was not his strong suit. (He has improved in this area over time!)

A few minutes later we kicked our shoes off and waded ankle deep into the water. Shawn had his arms around me as we stood together in silence. Eventually, I asked him what he was thinking, and without hesitating, he pulled the ring out of his pocket and officially asked the question I had been waiting to hear, "Will you marry me?" He slipped a gorgeous ring on my finger, and I was shocked by its extravagance! I had been anticipating a simple solitaire. Instead, I was wearing a white gold band with a sizeable diamond mounted on a setting that reminded me of a princess crown. Smaller diamonds lined the band on either side of the mounted diamond, and tiny diamonds were embedded in the mount itself. As we admired the sparkling ring, we decided to count all the diamonds. There were exactly twenty-seven. We were both shocked and thrilled because my birthday it May 27! It felt like one more little affirmation that God's hand was indeed over every detail of our relationship.

We were on an emotional high as we began announcing the news of our engagement with friends and family. It was August, and we had five months to plan our wedding. I was overwhelmed that the dream of my heart was about to become a reality!

19
I Am My Beloved's and He is Mine

As our wedding countdown commenced, there were times it felt as though our big day was quickly approaching, but at other times it felt like we were moving at a snail's pace. Our anticipation was so great! Since we were getting married around Christmas time, we decided to use the colors white, silver, and a deep satin red. I enjoyed every detail of the planning process, especially going to pick out a wedding dress. Shawn and I had agreed that he wouldn't see me on our wedding day until I walked down the aisle, but he did flip through the bridal dress catalogue I had ordered. There was a particular dress that had really caught my eye, but I kept this to myself, not taking the chance of ruining the surprise. I was secretly thrilled, though, when he commented on the same dress; it was one of his favorites as well!

The day came to actually shop for a dress with some of my girlfriends. I only tried on a couple because the one from the catalogue was hands down my favorite, especially after I saw it on me. I could hardly wait for Shawn to see me dressed as his bride!

Though we had a small wedding budget to work with, we received such an outpouring of love and support from friends. One man from our church practiced photography as a hobby and offered to take all of our engagement and wedding photos free of charge. We only had to pay for the film and development. We saw God's hand at work in everything, big and small. On the day we were scheduled to take our engagement pictures, we woke up to a sky that was gray, overcast, and windy. We were feeling discouraged because all of our pictures were going to be taken outdoors. We prayed, and when the time came for our photo shoot, the sun was shining, and the wind had disappeared. It was perfect weather for picture taking. However, an hour or so after our photo shoot was completed, the sky returned to being gray and overcast. I felt so incredibly loved in that moment!

Another couple from our church had previously owned a bridal shop. They offered to make my bouquet as well as all of the corsages and boutonnieres. Again, all we had to pay for was the cost of materials. The wife accompanied me to the craft store when the silk flowers were on sale, and helped me pick out the perfect ones! In addition, another friend of ours was a D.J. on the side. He offered to play all the music at our reception at no cost. My friend's mother offered to make homemade truffles for the reception, and a co-worker's sibling who did professional cake design, made all of our cakes at a discounted rate. The list went on and on. We were overwhelmed by the kindness and generosity of so many who helped to make our wedding day extra beautiful and extra special!

Finally, the big day arrived, December 18, 2005. Our wedding wasn't scheduled until early evening, and I knew I wouldn't see Shawn until we met at the altar. I was a ball of nervous excitement! That morning my sweet roommate, who was also my maid of honor, fixed me a delicious breakfast. Soon after, I headed off to the mall to meet up with my mom and mother-in-law for our hair appointments. From there my mom accompanied me to have my make-up professionally done. I felt like a princess!

I arrived at the church in the afternoon with my bridesmaids, and we finished getting ready so we could take some pictures. We decided to take as many pictures as possible prior to the wedding, only saving the couple and family shots for later. Once pictures we finished, it was the waiting game. The butterflies in my stomach continued to build as the time drew closer, and I could hear the sounds of guests arriving and soon the processional music beginning to play.

Before long I found myself waiting outside the sanctuary doors, preparing to see my beloved for the first time that day…

I described our wedding ceremony in the prologue, but I would now like to add the personal vows that Shawn and I shared with each other. We had each written them down privately, and Shawn was to go first. He nervously pulled out his paper, unfolded it, and attempted to smooth it out on the front of his tuxedo, ripping it in the process! Without giving the paper another look, he simply shared from his heart:

Dana, you know that I love you. I love you very much. I'm not always good with my words, so actually I'm planning to sing to you how I feel about you (dramatic pause as the bride giggles nervously), *but then realizing that everyone was here, I decided not to put them through it!* (the sanctuary erupts in laughter). *I really do love you. I don't have the exact words to express how I feel when I'm near you. There are some days when I feel really bad, but when I see you I have to smile. There are certain days I've had a normal day, and you come in, and I just want to dance around you! I don't have the words, but literally when you come into a room, and I see you, there's something that feels like it jumps inside of me. It's expectation. It's excitement, and I've never had that with anyone else. I really think that's what the Lord put in me, just between the two of us that no one else can have. I believe that my love for you is truly very genuine, and if it's genuine then I know it's from Him. If it's from Him that means it's between the two of us, and that makes you a treasured possession* (nervous pause). *I meant to say "GIFT" that I want to treasure!* (lots of laughter). *I was practicing to my best man last night. I'm nervous!* (more laughter). *I do, I want to treasure you. You are a gift the Lord has given. I know that He will give me grace to do that because I can't do that on my own. I love you* (choking back tears).

Teary-eyed, I opened up my vows and read what I had written from my heart as we both cried:

I've dreamed of this day my whole life, but my dreams never brought me even close to imagining the depth of love that's in my heart for you and the great honor I feel to be your partner in this life. You are a strong and compassionate man of God, and I am overwhelmed by the Lord's goodness that He chose you to be my husband and me to be your wife. It is my desire to love you, honor you, and serve you with all that is in me every day of our life together. I promise to love you second only to Jesus. I know He has wonderful things in store for us, and I look forward to learning with you and growing with you as we journey through this life. I love you so much, and I give you all my love this day and every day until Jesus calls us home.

The joy that filled both our hearts that day was so deep and full. We had a lovely reception with friends and family, and near the end I surprised Shawn by pulling out my guitar and playing an original song I had written just for him:

ALL MY LOVE

When I look into your eyes
I see glimpses of His love
When you hold me in your arms
I feel His warm embrace
To be with you can only be
A blessing from above
And I know the hand of Jesus
Has brought us to this place

All my love for all my life
I give to you today
And all my words cannot express
All that's in my heart to say

What a mystery it is
That two lives can be made one
What a joy to know together
We will serve the Lord our God
We are joined that we may be
A reflection of the Son
I am yours, we are His

We are purchased by His blood

All my love for all my life
I give to you today
And all my words cannot express
All that's in my heart to say
I never knew a love so sweet
Would come knocking on my door
Yet this is the beginning
Of all we have in store

All my love for all my life
I give to you today
And all my words cannot express
All that's in my heart to say

Soon it was time to finish saying our goodbyes and leave for our wedding night. The wait was over, and our consciences were clear. We have no regrets…

20
Dream Come True

At the time of this writing, it's been nearly ten years since Shawn and I entered into the beautiful covenant of marriage. In order to bring our story to a close, I decided to include the last chapter of my first book, <u>Reflections from Holland: A New Mother's Journey with Down Syndrome</u>.

What do you want to be when you grow up? This is a question that children are asked throughout their years of childhood, and their answers may change from year to year (or day to day) as they develop and mature. I remember the many answers I had to this question during my own growing up years: *singer, writer, teacher, actress, veterinarian* (only for a short time until I realized I would actually have to do things that involved blood and needles, not just play with animals all day)! While many things from this list still ring true to the passions of my heart, there is one answer that has always been deeply rooted inside of me, unchanging amid the many changes of childhood, adolescence, and adulthood. *What do you want to be when you grow up?—a* **Mommy***!*

As a teenager I would have told you that my ideal life scenario would be to marry a pastor and be a stay-at-home mom. I envisioned the beauty and romance of being married to a godly man and ministering together, raising adorable and well-behaved children, and being a model homemaker as I spent my days in the bliss of motherhood—reading books, singing songs, baking cookies, making crafts, playing imaginative games, etc…In my mind it was a picture of true contentment, my "happily ever after" if you will.

This was my dream at sixteen. At the time that I write this I am thirty-one, and by most outward appearances I am living my dream. I did marry a wonderful and godly man. In our early years of marriage we were involved in youth ministry together. For the last two years he has been ministering in a pastoral role at the small church we helped to plant. He also has the opportunity to pastor young hearts in his new job as special education teacher at one of our local middle schools. I love him and respect him, proud of the man he is and is becoming. I am privileged to be a stay-at-home mom for our two precious children and believe that in time there will be more to come. I do spend my days reading books, singing songs, rocking babies, cooking meals, keeping house, and the list goes on and on…

Yet in the midst of these blessings, I've had to come face to face with the restlessness of my own heart. For one thing, when I was sixteen I didn't take into account the amount of hard work and monotony that actually comes with maintaining a marriage, raising a family, keeping a home, and serving in ministry. I also didn't fully take into account that no dream fulfilled, no matter how beautiful or noble, can truly satisfy my heart—only Jesus can.

I was talking with my husband in the car awhile back and shared with him some of the struggles I was experiencing. I was feeling lonely in my role as a homemaker. I was feeling disappointed that I was limited in the activities I could be involved in, especially at our church. I was feeling discouraged thinking I was missing the mark in almost every area of my life. I felt like I was somehow "missing out." As is often his advice, Shawn exhorted me to ask the Lord for His perspective on things and allow Him to change my paradigm. Somewhere in the midst of this I recognized the irony of my own woes and had to laugh at myself. *You said you wanted to be a pastor's wife and homemaker. God has given you the desires of your heart!*

Recently the Lord has been bringing me wonderful encouragement concerning my role and calling as a mother. Some of it has been through the heartfelt writing of other moms, some has been through spoken testimonies, and some has been through His own whispered words to my heart. *But Jesus said, "Let the little children come to Me, and do not hinder them; for the kingdom of heaven belongs to such as these," (Matthew 19:14 NIV).* He has been lovingly reminding me of things I've known to be true but have sometimes lost sight of in the midst of the busyness and demands of each day. Mothers are given the extraordinary responsibility and privilege of raising the next generation of world changers. We are called to nurture, teach, and disciple the little ones who are to inherit the Kingdom of God. Our words and actions are forming our children's earliest framework for how they will view God; we are called to be a representation of His heart! We are entrusted with stewarding, for a season, the lives of the very ones who hold such immense value in His eyes. These are the ones He created, the ones He poured out His blood to redeem, and the ones who have been in His heart for all eternity. Motherhood is a high calling, but it is a calling that must be walked out in the ordinary, mundane, everyday issues of life. It is also a calling that can only be fulfilled as I set my heart to love and worship Jesus in midst of these very things. This is where true life and contentment is found.

We all have different dreams, but the truth is, no matter how big or small a dream may be, no matter how ordinary or extraordinary it appears, a dream in itself is powerless to bring lasting contentment, and it is ultimately meaningless if it is not rooted in relationship with Jesus Christ. There have been many great accomplishments in the eyes of man throughout history that will be forgotten in eternity. Yet there have been many simple, hidden lives, unnoticed by the world around, loving Jesus wholeheartedly and faithfully serving in the situations of everyday life that will be remembered and celebrated in heaven. This gives me great hope and renewed vision for how I want to live my life in this season and every season.

When I focus my heart on Jesus in simple love and worship as I sweep Cheerios off the floor multiple times a day, or as I change another dirty diaper, or as I sing "The Wheels on the Bus" for what seems like the hundredth time, it is noticed and remembered in heaven. When motivated by love for Him no task is insignificant, and it carries the promise of eternal reward. As I speak words of life and destiny into my children and shower them with love and affection as we walk through our very natural days, I am helping to paint a portrait for them of a supernatural God Who loves them crazy and has called them to be His own.

Yes, being a wife and mother is my dream come true, but the greatest dream of my heart is to be a whole-hearted lover of my Lord and Savior Jesus Christ, to grow in the knowledge of Him, and to represent Him in this world, living as He lived and loving as He loved. It is only in the pursuit of this dream that I can be the wife and mother He has called me to be. This is the dream that must consume all other dreams. This is my true dream of happily ever after!

21
Forgiveness and Repentance: The Two-Sided Coin

Having shared our story, I now want to I touch on the eternally significant realities of forgiveness and repentance. This will undoubtedly be my longest chapter; indeed, whole volumes could and have been written on these weighty matters. With my limited time and space, I hope to at least clearly communicate and encapsulate this subject about which I have become so passionate. The truths I am about to discuss are truly a matter of life and death pertaining to every person, and the choices made in these areas can open the door to either the greatest present and eternal blessings or the most devastating and lasting consequences. I am not being dramatic; I say this with complete seriousness and heart-felt conviction.

I believe that there has been a lack of understanding and teaching about what forgiveness truly is and what it is not. Forgiveness and, in time, repentance were the pivotal points in my journey of inner healing and breaking out of the destructive cycle I had wrestled with for so long. I wish that I had been taught these truths sooner; it could have saved me much grief. However, my prayer is that as I have shared from my own journey, and as I seek to clearly articulate these crucial matters, others will find themselves on a path of inner healing and greater freedom.

People who have been deeply hurt by others may cringe at the word "forgiveness," often because of a faulty understanding of what forgiveness truly means. So, let's start with what forgiveness is NOT:

Forgiveness is not a justification of the wrong that was done.

I have found that many people fear that if they forgive the person who has wronged them, they are somehow dismissing the wrong done against them as though it was okay. This is simply not true. People sin against us. We sin against others. Hurt people inevitably hurt people. When an action is wrong, it is wrong. Forgiveness does not undermine that reality. It *does*, however, release that person from any debt that we hold against them. It is in effect saying, "Though you wronged me, I release you from owing me anything. I leave you in God's hands."

Some people really struggle with this concept because it seems so unjust. As humans we hold a deep, inner demand for justice to be served. There should be a payment, a consequence for sins committed. What we must remember, though, is that the payment was already made on a cross over 2,000 years ago. Jesus died for the sins of all mankind. He took the penalty upon Himself so that there could be forgiveness. The truth is, without the sacrifice of the Son of God, we would all be eternally condemned. There is no way I could ever pay for the sin in my own life; I *need* God's forgiveness. Therefore, I will not expect others to pay for their sin against me. I will follow the example of my Savior and release forgiveness. In the very midst of the agonizing torture of the cross, Jesus prayed concerning his killers, *"...Father, forgive them, for they do not know what they do..."* (Luke 23:34).

Forgiveness is not always a feeling.

Many people struggle to forgive because they believe they must *feel* forgiveness towards the one who hurt them in order for it to be genuine. Countless times I have heard people confess, "I have tried to forgive them, but I still feel so hurt and angry. I guess I'm just not ready." If we are waiting to feel forgiveness towards the person who wronged us, we may never get there. Forgiveness is a *choice* long before it is a feeling. Forgiveness and healing do go hand-in-hand, but they are not the same thing. When I choose to forgive someone, I am opening the door to the prison I have been bound in, and I am making the way for God to lead me out and begin healing my heart. I have heard so many people say that forgiveness is a process, but I disagree with this statement, though I understand where they are coming from. Forgiveness is a **choice**; *healing* is a process, but neither of them will happen automatically. Time does not heal all wounds; Jesus does. *"He heals the brokenhearted and binds up their wounds"* (Psalm 147:3).

Forgiveness is not a sign of weakness.

The mindset that forgiveness is a sign of weakness is a great error. There is a misconception that if I hold onto my anger and bitterness towards another, I somehow have a measure of control. The reality, though, is that the anger and bitterness are actually controlling me. There is incredible strength in forgiveness because, in doing so, I am taking control of my own soul and bringing it into subjection, instead of allowing my circumstances and emotions to control me. The Eternal, All-Powerful, Creator of the universe demonstrated His strength through the cross of Jesus Christ. *"If You, Lord, should mark iniquities, O Lord, who could stand? But there is forgiveness with You, that You may be feared"* (Psalm 130:3). If God, Who is perfect and holy, extends forgiveness to us for our sins, who are we to withhold forgiveness from another?

Forgiveness is not optional.

That forgiveness is not optional is a very sobering reality. Countless people, including Christians, feel completely justified in their lack of forgiveness towards others. However, God makes it clear in His Word that we cannot be forgiven if we ourselves do not forgive. He does not state this once, but over and over again. He must think this is crucially important. I will include a few of those passages here.

In Matthew 18, Peter asks Jesus how often he should forgive someone who sins again him, putting the cap on seven times, which I'm sure seemed very generous to him. Jesus responds, *"...I do not say to you, up to seven times, but up to seventy times seven"* (Matthew 18:22). He then goes on to share a parable (see Matthew 18:23-35). He talks about a king who had a servant who owed him an unthinkable amount of money, one that would be impossible to pay. The king was going to punish the man for his debt, but the servant begged for mercy. The king had compassion on him and completely forgave his debt. Soon after the servant saw one of his fellow servants who owed him a sum of money, not even a drop in the bucket compared to the debt from which he had just been released. He demanded that the man pay him back right then. The fellow servant did not have the means to pay at that time and begged for mercy, just as he had done. However, instead of showing compassion, the servant threw the man in prison until his debt could be paid. When the king heard about the incident, he was enraged at the audacity of the servant to hold another in debt when he had just been released from so much. Jesus ends the parable with these sobering words, *"And his master was angry, and delivered him to the torturers until he should pay all that was due to him. So My heavenly Father also will do to you if each of you, from his heart, does not forgive his brother his trespasses"* (Matthew 18:34-35).

When we refuse to forgive another, we literally open ourselves up to great torment. Some of the most miserable people I know are those who are bitter and unforgiving towards others. The refusal to forgive others is an insult to the incredible grace of God and a sign of great arrogance. We have been offered the greatest forgiveness imaginable; freedom from a debt we could never pay. If we do not in turn extend forgiveness to others, we might as well hand Satan a key to our front door, because we have given him legal access to come in and wreak havoc in our lives.

The consequences of unforgiveness not only affect this earthly life, but our eternal destiny hinges on our choices in this area as well. This is a strong statement, but I believe it is a biblical one. In Matthew 6, the disciples asked Jesus how they should pray. Many are familiar with the Lord's Prayer, but do we really take the words of it to heart? *"And forgive us our debts, as we forgive our debtors"* (Matthew 6:12). Sometimes we breeze right over Jesus' words at the completion of this prayer, but to do so is very dangerous indeed. *"For if you forgive men their trespasses, your heavenly Father will also forgive you. But if you do not forgive men their trespasses, neither will your Father forgive your trespasses"* (Matthew 6:14-15). I cannot obtain grace for my own life while at the same time demanding punishment for another. If I want to be forgiven, I **must** forgive. I cannot be in right relationship with God without it: *"And whenever you stand praying, if you have anything against anyone, forgive him, that your Father in heaven may also forgive you your trespasses"* (Mark 11:25).

By establishing what forgiveness *is not*, we have also established that *forgiveness is:*
- *A command*
- *An obedient act of the will*

- ***Essential for inner healing to take place...and...***

Forgiveness is also a lifestyle.

The Christian life is not a one-time prayer at the altar. It is a daily lifestyle of drawing closer to the heart of God and living our lives in obedience to Him. The same principal applies to forgiveness. This understanding is crucial, and in this sense forgiveness is an ongoing process. When I first made the decision to forgive my dad, it was not a one-time event. Every time a new layer of pain or anger would surface or a new wound would be inflicted, I would turn my heart to the Lord and pray, "Father, I choose to forgive my dad for..." When Jesus gave Peter the command of continuous forgiveness in Matthew 18, He meant it. Sometimes, we have to choose forgiveness multiple times a day. When you are on a journey of inner healing, you may have to re-affirm your decision to forgive over and over and over. This does not mean that you have been unsuccessful in forgiving; it means that you are creating a lifestyle that does not allow for bitterness and resentment to take root and remain. Jesus tells us in Matthew 18:7 that offenses will come; they are an inevitable part of living in a fallen world. However, our response to offenses is what matters most. As long as we live in this world, we will be given daily choices to take offense or to release forgiveness in matters both great and small. The choice is always up to us.

"Therefore, as the elect of God, holy and beloved, put on tender mercies, kindness, humility, meekness, longsuffering; bearing with one another, and forgiving one another, if anyone has a complaint against another; even as Christ forgave you, so you also must do" (Colossians: 3:12-13).

Now let's take a look at the other side of the coin—repentance. Whenever we have made bitter judgments against another, there must be repentance in that area. *"Judge not, that you may not be judged. For with what judgment you judge, you will be judged; and with the measure you use, it will be measured by to you"* (Matthew 7:1-2). When Jesus teaches us not to judge, He is speaking about the *spirit* in which we judge. I think there is often misunderstanding in this area. We are to correctly judge between right and wrong (i.e. It is a correct judgment to say that stealing is wrong). However, there is a great difference between judging a *behavior* and judging a *person*. It is the judgment against a person made from a critical spirit that Jesus is addressing. We live in a society that trumpets, "Don't judge!" yet many people walk through life with a critical and accusing attitude towards others in all matters great and small. This state of being often springs from hurts that have never been dealt with that are deeply rooted in bitterness.

As I delve into explaining this vital key to healing, allow me share a bit more from my own story. Here is a personal example: I started choosing to forgive my dad while I was in college. However, I was still repeating many of the negative patterns in my life, and getting pulled into relationships with guys who had similar struggles to my dad, though I couldn't see it at the time. In my pain over the years, I had unknowingly formed bitter judgments against my dad that led to inner vows I made to myself. In my pain I criticized him in my heart, judging him from a place of anger and feeling fully justified in doing so. I made vows to myself such as, "I will never marry someone like my dad." "I will never let myself get hurt like my mom did." Yet, here I was setting myself up for a similar cycle over and over again. It was as though the very thing I wanted to avoid was the very thing that kept following me in my life. Forgiveness wasn't enough. I had to choose repentance.

I want to quote an excerpt from an excellent little booklet by John and Carol Arnott entitled "What Christians Should Know About…The Importance of Forgiveness." I wish every Christian had this teaching in their hands:

> If there are areas in your life where repetitive, negative things keep happening; if there are areas where you are unable to love someone as you should; look back and say, "Holy

> Spirit, will you show me? Will you reveal it to me if I have judged a primary person in my life? Have I dishonored him or her?"
> You may not be in touch with your anger, hurt and emotions. You may have no recollection of ever judging anyone, but if repetitive, negative fruit is in your life, there is usually a judgment rooted in bitterness, anger or hurt, that is allowing the enemy access.[14]

Some of us come from homes full of loving family values, while others of us come from homes full of pain and dysfunction. Whatever our experiences have been, though, one thing is sure. None of us have had perfect parents. They all mess up at times and make mistakes. The hidden wounds that continue to plague the lives of adults are often deeply rooted in childhood pain. Here's a bit more from the Arnotts:

> The Scripture says to honor your father and your mother only if they are good Christians and if they do everything right. Oops. No, it doesn't say that, does it? Don't you wish? ... No, it says,
> *Honor your father and your mother, as the Lord your God has commanded you, so that you may live long and that it may go well with*

you in the land the Lord your God is giving you. (Deuteronomy 5:16)

Conversely, in the areas in which you dishonor them, it will not go well with you. We do not judge them in every area, of course, but we judge and dishonor them in the areas where we have been hurt and neglected.[15]

Did my dad make mistakes? Yes. Did he hurt me in the process? Yes. However, the fact was I had still dishonored him in my heart through my bitter judgment, and I had given the enemy legal access to bring destruction into my life in that area. One of life's hardest lessons to learn is that, regardless of how I have been wronged by another, I still have personal responsibility over how I respond. Often, the greater the hurt inflicted, the greater the bitter judgment made, and the greater the need for forgiveness and repentance so that we can reap blessings in our lives instead of curses. Just as forgiveness does not justify another person's behavior but releases them from their debt to us, repentance does not undermine the fact that we have been hurt but takes responsibility for our own wrong response.

In my own life, accessing the keys of forgiveness and repentance has ushered in great healing, freedom, and blessing. I shudder to think of where my life would be right now if I chose instead to hold onto my bitterness and judgment. I don't think I would be enjoying the happy and stable marriage I feel to privileged to be a part of. My heart is also much more tender towards God and towards my dad. Though I have not seen him for nearly fifteen years at the time of this writing, our long distance relationship is healthier that it's ever been. I have genuine love and compassion in my heart towards him, and I can recognize how deeply God has been at work in his life over the last few decades. I have also been on an incredible journey of discovering God's heart as a loving and attentive Father. His love has brought such profound healing to the deep places of pain in my heart.

    I encourage you, whatever pain or trauma you have experienced in your life, give it to Jesus. Allow Him to lead you down the road of forgiveness, repentance, and healing. There is greater joy and freedom waiting for you!

22
Healing Prayers

Perhaps you are realizing that there are people in your life whom you need to forgive and that you need to repent for areas of judgment against them. Perhaps that person is even you. Just as we cannot hold others in unforgiveness and judgment, we cannot hold ourselves there either. I want to take a moment to offer some simple prayers to help you begin your own journey of healing. There is nothing special about the words I use, but sometimes it's difficult to know where to begin when dealing with the deep issues of our hearts. I encourage you to allow these prayers to be a springboard for you to begin your own dialogue with the Father in heaven who loves you so immensely!

If you have heard about Jesus but never surrendered your heart to Him and received His grace and forgiveness, this must be your starting point. We cannot give to another something we have not received ourselves. If you want to receive Him now, or if you feel like you walked with Him at one point in your life but have drifted away, please pray this with me…

Father, thank You for loving me so much that You sent Your only Son to die on the cross for my sins. Jesus, thank You for Your love for me and for Your obedience to Your Father to lay down Your life in my place that I may be saved. I confess that I am a sinner in need of Your forgiveness. I believe that You took the penalty of my sin when you gave your life on the cross, and I believe that You rose again three days later, defeating the power of sin and death. I ask You right now to forgive me of my sins and to come in and be Lord of my life. Fill me with the Holy Spirit and teach me Your ways. Thank You that I am now a new creation in Christ, and You empower me to live in a new way. I pray this in Jesus' name.

If you prayed this prayer from your heart, you are truly forgiven in Christ, and a brand new life has been opened up to you! I encourage you to tell someone today about the decision you have made and get connected with a church where you can build relationships with other Christians. We were made for relationship with God and each other, and we cannot live the Christian life alone.

If you are ready to make the choice to walk in forgiveness towards those who have hurt you, please pray this with me…

*Father, right now I choose to forgive **(name or names of those you need to forgive)** for **(be specific about what you need to forgive them for)**. Please forgive me for holding unforgiveness in my heart toward them. I release **(name/s)** to you right now. I declare that they owe me nothing. I entrust them to Your hands, and I pray that You would work in their lives. I thank You that Your grace gives me the power to forgive. I invite You to heal my heart where it's been broken. I pray this in Jesus' name.*

Now it's time for the other side of the coin: repentance…

*Father, I repent right now for holding bitter judgment and criticism in my heart towards **(name/s)**. I have judged them for **(be specific)**. Forgive me for dishonoring them. I renounce any inner vows I have made over my life in response to my hurt and anger.* ***(Be specific about any inner vows you have made; ie. "I'll never be like…")***. *I plead the shed blood of Jesus over my heart and life. Break the power of any* *curse that has been operating in my life on account of judgment and release Your blessing in those areas instead. Reveal to me any lies I have believed about myself and show me the truth that will replace those lies in my heart and mind. Thank You that You are a God of restoration. I pray this in Jesus' name.*

If you have prayed any of these prayers, I encourage you to take some time to just be quiet in the Lord's Presence and ask Him to speak to your heart. It may help you to play some soft music and to have a journal on hand to write down anything that comes to your mind. Usually in every place that we have been hurt a lie has come in and taken root in our hearts. These lies must be identified and renounced, and we must allow the Holy Spirit to show us the truth that will replace the power of the lie. An example might be if you have experienced a lot of rejection in your life. The lies that could have taken root in you may be that you will always be rejected or that you are not loveable. As you release these lies to the Lord and ask Him for the truth, He may speak to your heart that He has always wanted You, and that you bring Him joy. Again, these are just examples. The important thing is to be in His Presence and allow Him to speak to you.

Remember that the choice to forgive is the first step in a journey toward inner healing. You will have to daily make choices to forgive and to repent for any areas that God shows you there has been judgment. Make daily time to be in His Presence, and allow Him to bring things up. You don't need to try to dig things up yourself. Let Him take you by the hand and lead you through the healing process. It may help to have a few trusted Christians who you can confide in and ask them to pray for/with you as you walk this out.

I want to pray a prayer of blessing over you...

Father, I thank You for the ones holding this book right now. I thank You that you know every detail of their lives. You are familiar with every place of pain and You desire to bring full healing and restoration. I thank You that You are close to the broken-hearted and save those who have been crushed in spirit. I bless the ones reading this right now. Holy Spirit, come upon them and release the peace of Jesus. Take them deeper into Your heart of love and give them the strength and resources they need to walk out their healing and to step into the destiny of the Lord over their lives. I pray this in Jesus' name.

23
A Night for Grace

(While in the process of writing this book, I composed the following short story for a creative writing contest at our local public library. The story line is inspired by our own story as well as my daydream for our young daughter Joelle in years to come. I was pleasantly surprised when my piece was awarded first place for the category of adult fiction. It seemed only fitting to include it here!)

Grace twirled in front of her bedroom mirror in her brand new dress, checked to make sure her hair and make-up were just right, and smiled wide. Tonight was a very special night. She had celebrated her fourteenth birthday a few days prior, and this evening she was going on her very first date with a very special someone. Butterflies of excited anticipation fluttered in her stomach as she grabbed her purse and bag and got ready to head downstairs for her big night. She had been instructed to dress up for dinner but have a change of comfy clothes ready for activities later in the evening. As she descended the staircase, her date was waiting for her at the bottom, dressed in suit and tie, holding a bouquet of red roses and beaming with a huge smile spread across his face. As she reached his side, he bent down, gently kissed her on the cheek, and whispered, "You look beautiful, Princess!"

"Thank you, Daddy," Grace giggled. "The flowers are gorgeous!"

"I'll put them in a vase for you, Honey," her mother said smiling. "And now you two stand together so I can get a picture!"

A few minutes later the pair exited the house and headed for the car. Grace's dad opened the door for her as she slid in, shutting it gently behind her. "I've been looking forward to this evening for a long time," he said as he put the car in gear and pulled out of the driveway. "Let's go make some memories!"

Grace let out a gasp of delight about ten minutes later when they pulled into the parking lot of the nicest restaurant in town. Patrons could only dine there if they had made prior reservations. The candlelit tables were set with beautiful linen and fine china. The service staff members were all dressed in their best, ready to wait hand and foot on their customers. Grace had only driven by this high end place but had never dreamed of eating there. "We're having dinner here?!" she exclaimed.

"Only the best for my princess," her father replied with a grin.

They received a warm greeting from the staff as they entered and confirmed their reservations for the evening. As they were led back to their table set by a beautiful bay window, Grace noticed the hanging chandeliers, the lovely flower arrangements, and the small, live orchestra playing softly in the background. She was already feeling like a princess!

"Grace, please order anything you want on the menu. What looks good?" There were so many tempting options, but she finally decided on a savory grilled chicken dish, with creamy mashed potatoes, a generous tossed salad and steaming homemade bread rolls. Her dad ordered a juicy steak just the way he liked it with a delicious assortment of sides as well.
After their order was taken, and they waited for their dinner to arrive, Grace commented "Daddy, this place is beautiful! Thank you so much for bringing me here."

"It's my pleasure!" he replied. "Tonight is a special night, and I want you to feel just how valuable you are to me." They continued their conversation through their delicious dinner talking about Grace's school, her upcoming music and sports events, her friends, their family and anything else that popped up.

They laughed together, shared from the heart, and had a wonderful time. For dessert, they split a piece of decadent chocolate cake.

As they finished their meal and the dishes were cleared from the table, Grace's father shifted the conversation. "Grace, as I already mentioned, tonight is a very special night. I want you to know that your mom and I are so proud of you! You are growing up to be a beautiful young woman, inside and out. Thank you for allowing me the privilege of taking you on your first date."

"Daddy, thank *you* for taking me out tonight. You've made me feel so special!"

"You are special, Grace, and that's what I want to demonstrate to you tonight. I want you to remember that you deserve and should expect to be treated like a lady. You are entering a new season of your life, and I want you to know that your heart and your body are valuable gifts to be saved for the man who will one day commit to making you his wife. We have been praying for him since the day you were born, praying that he will be a man of love, integrity and purity—a man who will respect you and cherish you for life.

Smiling and teary-eyed Grace replied "Daddy, tell me again the story of how you and Mom fell in love."

"Gladly!" he said smiling. "As you know, we met while we were in college. It seemed we kept running into each other on campus. I recognized that she was a beautiful woman, but at that point I wasn't on the look-out for a relationship. I was focused on my studies and enjoying my time as a single. She wasn't looking for a relationship at that time either. However, with each encounter, we found that there was such an ease for conversation, and we really enjoyed each other's presence. In time, our "chance" encounters became planned encounters as a friendship began to grow. We spent time with groups of friends, but we also took walks around campus, or hung out at the local coffee shop talking about anything and everything. We were quickly becoming the best of friends, and it wasn't long before I realized that I was falling in love with this amazing woman. After having a serious heart-to-heart one night, I made a call to her parents the next day, requesting permission to date their daughter."

"Why did you ask permission, Daddy? Weren't you both old enough to decide for yourselves?"

"We were, but we wanted to invite our families into our developing relationship. I wanted to honor your mom by honoring her parents who had raised her. If she was to become my partner for life, I knew I would also be joined to her family as well. This is a big reason why we have such a close relationship with your grandparents today!"

"What was it like when you started dating?" Grace asked.

"It was exciting and a bit surreal as well. We had developed such a close friendship, and now we were trying to transition into something even deeper. We made a decision together early on that many people may not understand or even agree with. It wasn't a decision we *had* to make; it was a decision we *chose* to make. We agreed that we would save our first kiss for our wedding day, and if it turned out that we didn't marry, we could gracefully walk away from the relationship, knowing that we hadn't given that part of our hearts away."

"Why did you want to wait to kiss each other? Would it have been wrong to kiss?" Grace inquired.

"No, it wouldn't have been wrong. For us it wasn't about right or wrong but about better or best. We felt that the best decision for us was to wait, even for a kiss. We had both been in previous relationships where we had kissed. We knew that kissing awakened physical passion in a greater way, and we knew that we gave a piece of our hearts away with each kiss. We both carried regret and some painful memories from those earlier relationships. We wanted to protect ourselves and each other from further regret, should our relationship not end in marriage. As I said before, your mom is a beautiful woman, and of course I desired her. I also respected her and valued her. Protecting her heart and her purity was very important to me, and she felt the same way. We weren't keeping something *from* each other, but saving something *for* each other when it could be given its full expression in commitment and purity. I knew she was worth the wait!"

"Wasn't it still really hard to do? Some of my friends have boyfriends and they kiss. They tell me how romantic it is and how good it makes them feel."

"There were times it was hard, but since we made the decision together, it was much easier than most people would imagine. During the time we dated, we continued to focus mainly on our friendship, not on physical expressions of affection. Even after I proposed to her and we began making our wedding plans we continued to wait. We knew that the closer we came to our wedding day, the greater our desire for each other would become. We were committed to maintaining our virginity for our wedding night, and we didn't want to add needless temptation in this area. It's also important to recognize that sometimes physical connection can become a substitute for relational connection. It can make you feel so close to a person. It can make you feel like you really know them; but if there isn't genuine friendship as a foundation, it can be very misleading. If we had brought greater levels of physical affection into our relationship as we dated, we may have focused more on that than on our friendship. Your mom and I were best friends before we started dating and our friendship only continued to grow; we are still best friends today. Romantic feelings come and go in every relationship, but friendship is enduring."

Grace paused for a moment, considering what her dad just shared before asking, "What was it like when you finally kissed?"

Smiling, he replied, "It was one of the most incredible moments of my life! When your mom entered the church sanctuary, she took my breath away. She was the most beautiful bride I could have ever imagined. I could hardly focus on the wedding ceremony; I was so captivated by her! When the time came for us to seal our marriage with a kiss, I felt like my heart was going to beat out of my chest. Our first kiss was one of the most beautiful, memorable moments of my life. It's a memory I will always cherish. I know your friends have told you about how special it is when they kiss their boyfriends, but special moments now can become painful memories in the future if those relationships don't last. Every time you kiss, you offer a piece of your heart. It's important that the one you give this precious gift to is one who can be trusted with your heart, not someone just using you for their own momentary pleasure."

Grace was silent again as she let her father's words sink in.

"Grace, please understand that I am not telling you what you *have* to do. You will be responsible to make your own choices in this area. However, I do want to *encourage* you to make decisions that will benefit you and your future husband and protect you from needless pain. You may decide to approach the area of dating differently than your mom and I did, and you have the freedom to make that choice. Whatever you choose to do in time, I just want you to remember that your purity is a gift, and only you can choose who will open it. I know that you've committed before to saving your virginity for your marriage, and that commitment is a priceless one. We just celebrated your birthday, but there's one more gift that was saved especially for tonight!" With that, he reached into his pocket, pulled out a small velvet box, and gently handed it to his daughter.

"What's this?" Grace asked with surprise and delight in her eyes.

"Open it."

Grace carefully opened the small box and gasped. Inside was a beautiful white gold ring with a heart at the center outlined in delicate emerald stones—her birthstone. "Daddy! It's gorgeous!" she exclaimed.

Smiling, he gently removed the ring and slipped it on her left ring finger. "Grace, this is your purity ring. It is a representation of your commitment to God, yourself, and your future husband to save your virginity for your marriage bed. One day it will be replaced by a wedding ring from the man who will commit to you and cherish you for life. Your mom also received a purity ring as a teenager. She presented it to me as a gift on our wedding night. I cherish that ring and what it represents to this day."

"Daddy, I don't know what to say," Grace replied as she gazed at the sparkling ring on her finger. "This means so much to me! I will wear it every day."

Grace's dad looked at his daughter affectionately and said, "Honey, I am so very proud of you! You are such a treasure to me, and you will be a treasure to your husband someday… But that day is still a ways off, and we're not done with *our* date! What do you say we get changed, and I challenge you to a game of miniature golf?!"

"Absolutely," Grace responded, "but you know that I can beat you!"

"We'll see when we get there!"

An hour later Grace jumped up and down excitedly yelling, "Go, go, go!...Yes! I got a hole in one!"

"Okay," her dad conceded. "You beat me on that one, but we still have half the course to go. I still have a few tricks up my sleeve!" He pulled her into a side hug and planted a kiss on her forehead before heading to the next hole.

Giggling, Grace looked down again at her beautiful new ring, shimmering as the emeralds caught the light. "Yes," she thought, "I do want to save myself for a man who will cherish me, a man who honors me and values my purity, a man whom I can trust with my heart…a man just like Daddy!"

End Notes

1. Joshua Harris, *I Kissed Dating Goodbye* (Colorado Springs, CO: Multnomah Books, A Division of Random House, Inc., 1997, 2003), 9-10.
2. Ibid., 28.
3. Ibid., 19.
4. Ibid., 38-46.
5. Ibid., 50-53.
6. Debby Jones and Jackie Kendall, *Lady in Waiting* (Shippensburg, PA: Treasure House, An Imprint of Destiny Image® Publishers, Inc., 1995, 2000), 10.
7. Ibid., 40.
8. Ibid., 106.
9. Elisabeth Elliott, *Passion and Purity* (Grand Rapids, MI: Fleming H. Revell, A Division of Baker Book House Company, 1984), 59-60.
10. Ibid., 89.
11. Ibid., 113.
12. Joshua Harris, *I Kissed Dating Goodbye* (Colorado Springs, CO: Multnomah Books, A Division of Random House, Inc., 1997, 2003), 88.
13. Debby Jones and Jackie Kendall, *Lady in Waiting* (Shippensburg, PA: Treasure House,

An Imprint of Destiny Image® Publishers, Inc., 1995, 2000), 88.
14. John Arnott, *What Christians Should Know About...The Importance of Forgiveness* (Tonbridge, Kent TN11 0ZS, England: Sovereign World Limited, 1997), 32.
15. Ibid., 28.

About the Author

Dana Hemminger grew up in the Midwest, born in Missouri and raised in Kansas. At age 18 she moved to Bartlesville, OK to attend Oklahoma Wesleyan University where she studied behavioral science. Her interests during her school years included music, acting, and writing. She graduated from OWU in 2004 and married her best friend Shawn at the end of 2005. After spending four years working in the behavioral health field and Christian education, Dana was eager to take on the role of stay-at-home mom upon the birth of their first child Benjamin in 2009. In 2013 they welcomed their daughter Joelle into the world followed by their second son Josiah in 2015. Shawn and Dana have been on the pastoral team of a small church plant named The International House of Prayer-Bartlesville since 2011. Dana continues to express her creativity through writing, song and motherhood.

Made in the USA
Columbia, SC
18 July 2023